Genocide

Other Books of Related Interest:

At Issue Series

Casualties of War

Weapons of War

Current Controveries Series

Developing Nations

The Middle East

Introducing Issues with Opposing Viewpoints Series

Terrorism

Torture

Violence

Issues That Concern You Series

War

Opposing Viewpoints Series

War Crimes

GLOBALVIEWPOINTS

Genocide

Margaret Haerens, Book Editor

GREENHAVEN PRESS
A part of Gale, Cengage Learning

GALE
CENGAGE Learning·

Detroit • New York • San Francisco • New Haven, Conn • Waterville, Maine • London

Elizabeth Des Chenes, *Director, Publishing Solutions*

© 2012 Greenhaven Press, a part of Gale, Cengage Learning

Gale and Greenhaven Press are registered trademarks used herein under license.

For more information, contact:
Greenhaven Press
27500 Drake Rd.
Farmington Hills, MI 48331-3535
Or you can visit our Internet site at gale.cengage.com

For product information and technology assistance, contact us at

Gale Customer Support, 1-800-877-4253
For permission to use material from this text or product, submit all requests online at
www.cengage.com/permissions

Further permissions questions can be emailed to permissionrequest@cengage.com

Articles in Greenhaven Press anthologies are often edited for length to meet page requirements. In addition, original titles of these works are changed to clearly present the main thesis and to explicitly indicate the author's opinion. Every effort is made to ensure that Greenhaven Press accurately reflects the original intent of the authors. Every effort has been made to trace the owners of copyrighted material.

Cover image copyright © Ocean/Corbis.

LIBRARY OF CONGRESS CATALOGING-IN-PUBLICATION DATA

Genocide / Margaret Haerens, book editor.
    p. cm. -- (Global viewpoints)
    Includes bibliographical references and index.
    ISBN 978-0-7377-5652-4 (hardback) -- ISBN 978-0-7377-5653-1 (paperback)
    1. Genocide--Case studies. 2. Genocide--History. I. Haerens, Margaret.
    HV6322.7.G4465 2012
    364.15'1--dc23
                                                          2011051627

Printed in Mexico
1 2 3 4 5 6 7 16 15 14 13 12

Contents

Chapter 1: Recognizing and Defining Genocide

Many people in Israel believe that the Holocaust is unique and cannot be compared to any other incidents of genocide in history. Such a belief is immoral and does not stand the test of reason. It also isolates Jewish people from history and current events, as well as instills a sense of superiority and a lack of moral responsibility in the global community. Jewish students need to be taught universal lessons about discrimination, racism, oppression, and their role in fighting injustice.

More and more countries around the world are showing the political courage to officially recognize Turkey's genocidal campaign against the Armenian people that lasted from 1915 to 1923. In Turkey, there is an obsessive and hysterical denial of the long-proven facts of the atrocities. Turkey's threats against any person or country that dares to speak the truth about the Armenian genocide must stop. It must confront its own horrible actions and tell the truth about the past in order to move forward and take its place in the European Union.

Chapter 2: Contemporary Accounts of Genocide

Genocidal attacks of ethnic Nubians are being carried out by northern Sudanese forces in South Kordofan, a region in North Sudan. The ethnic Nubians sided with South Sudan, which successfully gained its independence from the North in 2011. North Sudan leaders claim that it is putting down a rebellion of ethnic Nubian insurgents; aid workers and other observers argue that the ethnic Nubians are being systematically massacred by government forces.

Chapter 3: Preventing and Prosecuting Genocide

In 2005 the United Nations endorsed the Right to Protect (R2P) doctrine, which allows the international community to take military action to prevent or stop mass violence within a state when the national government is unwilling or unable to do so. Unfortunately, in some cases, such as Darfur and the Democratic Republic of the Congo, it has failed to do so. Canada can be essential in reforming the process and making R2P more effective.

Chapter 4: The Legacy of Genocide

The chronic lawlessness that has allowed Guatemala's drug gangs to flourish can be traced back to a legacy of war crimes, widespread human rights violations, and genocide by US-backed government troops and militias in the late twentieth century. By the time peace accords were signed in 1996, Guatemala was hobbled by a corrupt ruling elite, weak and crooked government institutions, and law enforcement organizations that were doing business with drug gangs. The drug gangs quickly filled that power vacuum and now have complete power in some areas.

Foreword

*"The problems of all of humanity can
only be solved by all of humanity."*
—*Swiss author Friedrich Dürrenmatt*

Global interdependence has become an undeniable reality. Mass media and technology have increased worldwide access to information and created a society of global citizens. Understanding and navigating this global community is a challenge, requiring a high degree of information literacy and a new level of learning sophistication.

Building on the success of its flagship series, Opposing Viewpoints, Greenhaven Press has created the Global Viewpoints series to examine a broad range of current, often controversial topics of worldwide importance from a variety of international perspectives. Providing students and other readers with the information they need to explore global connections and think critically about worldwide implications, each Global Viewpoints volume offers a panoramic view of a topic of widespread significance.

Drugs, famine, immigration—a broad, international treatment is essential to do justice to social, environmental, health, and political issues such as these. Junior high, high school, and early college students, as well as general readers, can all use Global Viewpoints anthologies to discern the complexities relating to each issue. Readers will be able to examine unique national perspectives while, at the same time, appreciating the interconnectedness that global priorities bring to all nations and cultures.

Material in each volume is selected from a diverse range of sources, including journals, magazines, newspapers, nonfiction books, speeches, government documents, pamphlets, organization newsletters, and position papers. Global Viewpoints is truly global, with material drawn primarily from international sources available in English and secondarily from US sources with extensive international coverage.

Features of each volume in the Global Viewpoints series include:

- An **annotated table of contents** that provides a brief summary of each essay in the volume, including the name of the country or area covered in the essay.

- An **introduction** specific to the volume topic.

- A **world map** to help readers locate the countries or areas covered in the essays.

- For each viewpoint, an **introduction** that contains notes about the author and source of the viewpoint explains why material from the specific country is being presented, summarizes the main points of the viewpoint, and offers three "**guided reading questions** to aid in understanding and comprehension.

- **For further discussion** questions that promote critical thinking by asking the reader to compare and contrast aspects of the viewpoints or draw conclusions about perspectives and arguments.

- A worldwide list of **organizations to contact** for readers seeking additional information.

- A **periodical bibliography** for each chapter and a **bibliography of books** on the volume topic to aid in further research.

- A comprehensive **subject index** to offer access to people, places, events, and subjects cited in the text, with the countries covered in the viewpoints highlighted.

Global Viewpoints is designed for a broad spectrum of readers who want to learn more about current events, history, political science, government, international relations, economics, environmental science, world cultures, and sociology—students doing research for class assignments or debates, teachers and faculty seeking to supplement course materials, and others wanting to understand current issues better. By presenting how people in various countries perceive the root causes, current consequences, and proposed solutions to worldwide challenges, Global Viewpoints volumes offer readers opportunities to enhance their global awareness and their knowledge of cultures worldwide.

Introduction

"What connects two thousand years of genocide? Too much power in too few hands."

—Simon Wiesenthal,
an Austrian Holocaust survivor

In July 1995, the war between Serbs and Muslims near the town of Srebrenica in Bosnia took a tragic and bloody turn. For months, Bosnian Serbs had been fighting to secure territory in the Podrinje province, which was populated mainly by Bosnian Muslims, to establish a Serbian republic that was free of Muslim presence. To accomplish this, Serbian leaders in Bosnia implemented an ethnic cleansing campaign: When Serbian forces took a town or village, the military and police would come in and burn down Muslim homes, farms, and businesses. Bosnian Muslims would be forced to leave and find safety in Muslim-controlled areas. In many cases, Serb forces would torture and kill Muslim men, women, and children. The goal for Bosnian Serbs was a republic for Serbs, governed by Serbs.

Control of Srebrenica was key to that goal. In July 1995, however, Srebrenica was being protected by six hundred Dutch peacekeeping forces that were part of a North Atlantic Treaty Organization (NATO) effort. In 1993 Srebrenica was designated as a "safe area" by the United Nations (UN) Security Council, meaning that the area would be free of attacks or hostile acts from either party in the conflict. NATO troops were there to enforce it. From the beginning, both Serbs and Muslims violated the agreement: The Serb forces continued its attacks in the safe zone, and Muslim forces also launched attacks against Serbian areas. By July 1995, the situation deteriorated to the point that Bosnian Serb forces were openly attacking Srebrenica and the Dutch NATO forces. On July 11, 1995, Serb commander Ratko Mladic entered Srebrenica with his troops. The next day, an estimated twenty-three thousand Bosnian women and children were put on buses and deported from Srebrenica to Muslim-held territory. The men remained behind, ostensibly to be questioned by Bosnian Serb forces.

The next day the massacres began. Muslim men and boys were lined up and executed. Thousands of Bosnian Muslims—elderly men and women, mothers with babies, and small children among them—who had taken refuge at the Dutch battalion headquarters were handed over to Mladic's forces in exchange for the release of fourteen Dutch peacekeepers. Many of the women were brutally raped and tortured; hundreds of children and babies were senselessly slaughtered; and once again, Bosnian Muslim men were taken from their families and were tortured and killed.

Over the next few days, several other massacres occurred in Srebrenica. It is estimated that more than eight thousand Bosnian Muslims were coldly and systematically murdered by Mladic's troops—mostly men, but also women, children, and the elderly. Approximately thirty thousand Bosnian Muslims were forcibly removed from their homes and expelled from Srebrenica. It didn't take long for word of the Srebrenica massacre to reach the international media. The Dutch forces observed helplessly much of the mass rapes, torture, and killing that took place around its headquarters. A number of Bosnian Muslims were able to escape through wooded areas and report the murderous actions of Bosnian Serb forces in Srebrenica.

Later that year, the Dayton peace agreement was signed, effectively ending the war. By that time, Mladic's troops had gone in and tried to cover up the mass graves, in some cases digging up and moving the bodies of victims to other sites to throw off the inevitable investigation of the genocide. In recent years, many of the remains have been identified through DNA analysis.

Later in 1995, Mladic was indicted as a war criminal by the International Criminal Tribunal for the former Yugoslavia for his actions at Srebrenica. As the top military general with command responsibility, he was the one who gave the orders for the Srebrenica genocide; he was charged with genocide, war crimes, and crimes against humanity. Mladic escaped capture, and he remained on the run for sixteen years. He was eventually caught on May 26, 2011, in Lazarevo, Serbia, and was approved for extradition to The Hague in Switzerland to stand trial for his crimes.

Serbia was also the first country in history to be found in breach of the convention on genocide established by the United Nations. In 2007, the case against Serbia was heard at the International Court of Justice (ICJ), the UN's highest judicial body. The ICJ ruled that "the acts committed at Srebrenica falling within Article II *(a)* and *(b)* of the Convention were committed with the specific intent to destroy in part the group of the Muslims of Bosnia and Herzegovina as such; and accordingly that these were acts of genocide, committed by members of the VRS [Bosnian Serb army] in and around Srebrenica from about 13 July 1995." However, the ICJ determined that Serbia was not directly responsible for or complicit in the genocide—but it failed to prevent it.

The case of Srebrenica illuminates many of the challenges faced by states and international communities when it comes to predicting, preventing, and prosecuting genocide. It is quite clear that peacekeepers and international officials failed to predict and prevent the mass killings in Srebrenica. Even with NATO troops on the ground, a horrible genocide occurred, resulting in the brutal deaths of more than eight thousand citizens. Fortunately, the international justice system has had success in tracking down and prosecuting those responsible for the genocide. Mladic's capture and trial for his alleged crimes provided justice to the thousands of victims in Srebrenica.

After the horrors of the Holocaust during World War II, the international community made a commitment to prevent and intervene in ongoing genocidal campaigns. Tragically, the system failed in Srebrenica. Scholars and activists insist that the Srebrenica legacy will be the lessons learned from that failure and the adjustments made to mechanisms and policies meant to predict and prevent similar massacres. As with other genocides in Rwanda and Darfur, the international community is honing its response to the perpetration of war crimes and genocidal acts to better protect people around the world.

The authors of the viewpoints presented in *Global Viewpoints: Genocide* discuss many of these challenges and focus on some of the strategies the international community has developed to prevent genocide. The information in this volume also explores the problems with recognizing and defining the act of genocide, chronicles several contemporary genocidal campaigns occurring in the world, and considers how many countries that have suffered genocide are dealing with the painful legacy.

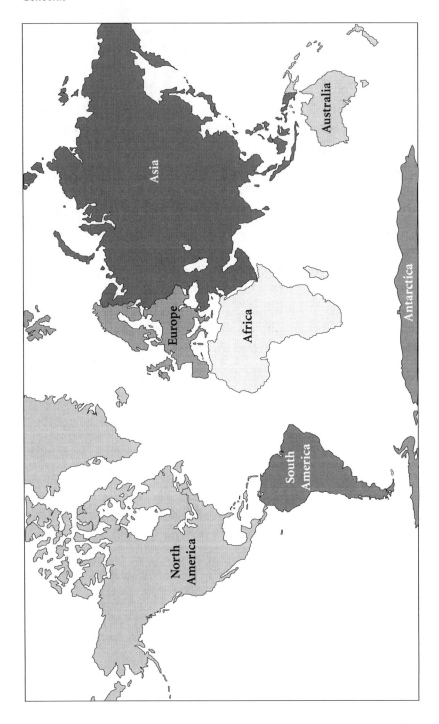

GLOBAL VIEWPOINTS

CHAPTER 1

Recognizing and Defining Genocide

The International Definitions of Genocide Are Being Challenged

Economist

The Economist *is a weekly newsmagazine. In the following viewpoint, the author outlines international attempts to define genocide, noting that the term is much more than a tool of historical or moral analysis—the word holds powerful political and legal ramifications that must be carefully considered before it is used for a specific situation. This has led judges and legal scholars to be cautious when applying the word, asserts the* Economist, *and has inspired historians and social scientists to widen the definition of genocide to include the destruction of indigenous cultures and languages, as well as the decimation of native people.*

As you read, consider the following questions:

1. How many people does the author say were victims of mass killing by the Khmer Rouge in Cambodia?

2. How many Muslim men and boys were killed near Srebrenica in Bosnia in 1995, according to official accounts?

3. Who does the author cite as the "prime mover" of the Convention on the Prevention and Punishment of the Crime of Genocide?

"The Uses and Abuses of the G-Word," *Economist*, June 2, 2011.

No less than the act itself, "the politics of genocide can be heartbreaking." That is what Sophal Ear, who fled Cambodia as a ten-year-old and now works as a politics professor in the United States, remembers feeling as a young man.

His father was among the 1.7 [million] victims of mass killing by the Khmer Rouge; by pretending to be a Vietnamese citizen, his mother spirited him and four other children to freedom. Yet before last year [2010], when four suspects were indicted for genocide, most murders by his homeland's Communist tyrants were not seen as genocidal in the legal sense, because killers and victims belonged to the same ethnic and religious group. Among the many crimes of Pol Pot's regime, only the killings of minorities like ethnic Vietnamese, or Muslims, fall neatly into the category of genocide.

Many people, faced with any of the scenes created by systematic slaughter during the 20th century would simply say: "I may not be a lawyer, but I know genocide when I see it." The reality of genocide may be easy to grasp at a gut level, yet its definition is complex. Prosecutors, judges, historians and politicians have made huge efforts in recent years to describe the boundaries of genocide: when mere mass murder stops and the ultimate human crime starts. Yet the term is far more than a tool of historical or moral analysis. Its use brings momentous political and legal consequences—and is therefore bound to be highly contested.

Such thinking pervaded bureaucratic debates in Washington, DC, in 1994 as news of massacres in Rwanda emerged. As Samantha Power, an author who works for President Barack Obama, has disclosed, a paper by a Pentagon official urged caution in using the G-word: "Be careful. . . . Genocide finding could commit [the government] to actually do something."

Plain Facts, Muddy Language

Even when the facts are clear, the vocabulary may not be. The killing of up to 8,000 Muslim men and boys near Srebrenica

Article 2 of the Convention on the Prevention and Punishment of the Crime of Genocide

In the present convention, genocide means any of the following acts committed with intent to destroy, in whole or in part, a national, ethnical, racial or religious group, as such:

• Killing members of the group;

• Causing serious bodily or mental harm to members of the group;

• Deliberately inflicting on the group conditions of life calculated to bring about its physical destruction in whole or in part;

• Imposing measures intended to prevent births within the group;

• Forcibly transferring children of the group to another group.

"Article 2,"
United Nations Convention on the Prevention
and Punishment of the Crime of Genocide,
December 9, 1948.

in Bosnia, in 1995, has been widely described as a genocidal act; that is why its alleged mastermind, the Bosnian Serb general, Ratko Mladic, was extradited to the Hague this week [June 2011]. Yet even in the Bosnian context, the word genocide has been challenged; prominent figures, who do not doubt the vileness of the war, raise questions about the proper legal category.

They include William Schabas, a Canadian law professor who heads the International Association of Genocide Scholars. He has stirred a furore by arguing that since many authorities reject the use of "genocide" to describe the whole military campaign by the Bosnian Serbs (or those of other war parties), it may not make sense to single out one episode in the war as genocidal; either there was a general bid to exterminate or there was not.

This thinking does not, he insists, diminish the horror of Srebrenica or of genocide-like acts in general. But he thinks the world should focus more on "crimes against humanity"— defined as killing and other inhumane acts when committed as "part of a widespread or systematic attack ... against any civilian population." Such felonious deeds should not be seen as a "discounted form of genocide" but as an extreme form of wickedness; they were, after all, the precise charges against the Nazis convicted at Nuremberg.

The special courts considering Rwanda and the Balkans have expanded the jurisprudence of both genocide and crimes against humanity.

International Efforts to Define Genocide

The starting point for any definition of genocide is clear and fairly familiar. The United Nations in 1948 adopted the Convention on the Prevention and Punishment of the Crime of Genocide, which describes "the deliberate and systematic destruction, in whole or in part, of an ethnical, racial, religious or national group." That formula is incorporated in the statutes of the Hague-based International Criminal Court [ICC], which since 2002 has stood ready to try terrible atrocities if national courts fail. In scores of countries the convention is also part of domestic law.

The prime mover of the convention, Raphael Lemkin, had been pressing since the 1930s for the adoption by world institutions of a broad ban on the mass slaughter of groups; he said later that he had been mainly motivated by the mass slaughter of Ottoman Armenians in 1915. The text was readily adopted in a climate of horror over the Nazi Holocaust of Jews as well as of Roma and other despised groups.

The convention's provisions are remarkable for what they do and do not cover. They exclude—at the insistence of the Soviet Union, for obvious reasons—the mass killing of "class" or political enemies. But they include as genocidal any measures to limit births within a group, and the transfer of children of one group to another. China's one-child policy would not count—because it applies to ethnic Chinese—unless it were brutally enforced on, say, Tibetans. Armenian nationalists enraged Mikhail Gorbachev, the then Soviet leader, by protesting over the adoption of orphans by Russians after the 1988 earthquake there. But they had law on their side.

The special courts considering Rwanda and the Balkans have expanded the jurisprudence of both genocide and crimes against humanity. The Rwanda one has stressed that the genocide charge requires proof of a plan, and that the victims were killed solely for membership of a group.

Trends in the Definition of Genocide

Mr Schabas sees two trends in the definition of genocide. First, judges and legal scholars have been cautious: The ICC judges, he points out, took a lot of persuading to issue an arrest warrant for genocide against Sudan's president Omar al-Bashir. Even the fact that they finally issued it does not mean they are persuaded that the G-word can stick. Meanwhile, social scientists and historians have widened the use of the word, to include, say, the destruction of cultures and languages, or the decimation of tribes. Indigenous peoples, for example, have died in big numbers because they were vulnerable to the diseases borne by colonisers. The effect is genocidal, whether or not there was a plan.

Judges and lawyers have to be precise because their opinions have precise effects: For historians, a perpetual testing and redefining of categories comes naturally. But that does not make the historian's work easy or free of heartbreaking consequences: witness the endless row over the mass killings of Armenians.

Only an open debate can resolve those questions. It does not help that asserting an Armenian genocide is a criminal offence in Turkey, whereas denying it is against the law in Switzerland. (France's lower house adopted a similar measure but was overruled in May by the Senate.) Arrest warrants may be the right way to deal with *genocidaires*, but they have no place in the study of history.

The United States Defines Genocide in a Way That Suits Its Interests

Rick Rozoff

Rick Rozoff is a journalist and the manager of Stop NATO. In the following viewpoint, he maintains that US politicians have employed and exploited the word genocide in order to fulfill their geostrategic objectives. Rozoff observes that the United States practices double standards by condemning governments it opposes and ignoring genocidal acts by allies. In addition, when the United States has perpetrated genocidal acts, those acts are presented to the world as constructive and necessary. US and international attempts to stop true acts of genocide end in more deaths, displacement, and exploitation of vulnerable people, Rozoff argues.

As you read, consider the following questions:

1. What does the author cite as examples of US genocidal acts, whether it be directly or in collusion with another country?

2. According to a study of Western media done by Edward S. Herman and David Peterson, in what manner did the media apply the word genocide in recent years?

3. What does the author classify as benign attempts to commit genocide?

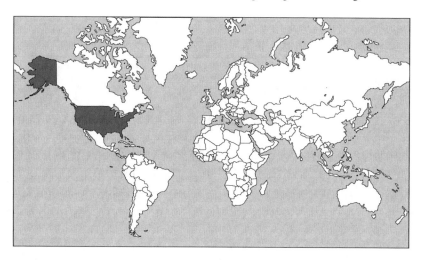

In 1895 novelist Anatole France—who in the same decade took up cudgels in defense of persecuted Armenians in the Ottoman Empire while also entering the lists on behalf of Alfred Dreyfus—wrote an essay in which he maintained that words are like coins. When freshly minted the images and inscriptions on them are clear. But by dint of constant circulation they become effaced until the outlines are blurred and the words unintelligible.

As Edward S. Herman and David Peterson write in *The Politics of Genocide*, "During the past several decades, the word 'genocide' has increased in frequency of use and recklessness of application, so much so that the crime of the twentieth century for which the word was originally coined often appears debased. Unchanged, however, is the huge political bias in its usage. . . ." With their painstaking efforts to compile information and analyze the self-serving misuse of this term by the government, media and establishment academic figures of the United States and its allies, the authors have performed a valuable service to the cause of truth and of peace.

The fact that combating "genocide" has replaced confronting communism in some notably left and liberal circles as a major intellectual and moral legitimation for an enduringly aggressive and interventionist U.S. foreign policy is not fortu-itous. It has been adopted to further American and allied in-terests in Europe and Africa in particular but with interna-tional application.

Genocide as Propaganda

Nowhere is this more explicit than in the U.S.-based Genocide Prevention Task Force's 2008 report "Preventing Genocide," where the "Save Darfur" activism of the last decade is singled out as a model for how to "build a permanent constituency for the prevention of genocide and mass atrocities."

But this shows that "Darfur has been . . . successfully framed as 'genocide,'" the authors counter, even as "the signa-ture nefarious bloodbath of the early twenty-first century," and we should take the task force's praise of "Save Darfur" ac-tivism to mean rather that the "U.S. establishment's handling of the western Sudan (ca. 2003–2010) should serve as a model for how best to propagandize a conflict as 'genocide,' and thus to mobilize elite and public opinion for action against its al-leged perpetrator."

The U.S. has rightly been accused of practicing double standards in relation to genocide charges.

During the past two decades, the post–Cold War era Wash-ington has employed and exploited the word genocide in fur-therance of geopolitical objectives in several strategic parts of the world. As the foreword to the volume by Noam Chomsky warns, the one-sided, nakedly partisan and frequently fact-distorting genocide stratagem not only diverts attention from genuine acts of mass killing and targeting of ethnic and other demographic groups perpetrated by the U.S., its allies and cli-ent states, but runs the risk of producing a boy who cried wolf effect, one moreover with a retroactive component.

Chomsky characterizes the authors' work as indicting a practice that since "the end of the Cold War opened the way to an era of virtual Holocaust denial." That is, as facts such as those marshaled by Herman and Peterson demonstrate, the exaggeration, distortion and even outright fabrication of genocide accusations may produce as an unintended consequence a universal scepticism on the matter, even—most alarmingly— toward the genuine article. That leveling charges of genocide against nations and governments the White House and State Department are opposed to, and in parts of the world where the Pentagon is bent on deploying troops . . . occurs as World War II revisionism, neo-Nazism and the formal rehabilitation of Nazi collaborators . . . is the most alarming manifestation of that disturbing phenomenon.

Double Standards

The U.S. has rightly been accused of practicing double standards in relation to genocide charges, condemning mass killings (alleged as well as real) in nations whose governments are not viewed favorably by Washington and its allies while ignoring, minimizing and justifying it when perpetrated by an approved government.

But it is not, as defenders of American foreign policy often state, a question of not being able to respond to every crisis or of responding to the most egregious situation first. Nor as the rapidly deteriorating Christopher Hitchens wrote in 1993 in one of his many efforts to mobilize opinion in favor of the "Bosnian cause" (by which he never meant anything beyond the Sarajevo Muslims around Alija Izetbegovic, and Hitchens' own mythic land of multiculturalism overrun by "racist" Serbs) is it a case of "making the best the enemy of the good."

Instead, as Herman and Peterson meticulously detail, it is a fixed policy of assigning cases and charges of genocide to four distinct categories, the first two applicable to the U.S. and its allies and clients, the second two to adversaries or other governments whose nations occupy space or possess resources coveted by Washington's empire builders and U.S.-based transnational corporations.

Drawing on years of observation and analysis of international events—in Herman's case efforts extending over five decades—the authors present a four-point model for examining how the issue of genocide is viewed by the American government, the mainstream news media and a veritable battalion of "engaged" academics and handsomely funded nongovernmental organizations (the latter sometimes not so nongovernmental).

As they explain:

"When we ourselves commit mass-atrocity crimes, the atrocities are Constructive, our victims are unworthy of our attention and indignation, and never suffer 'genocide' at our hands—like the Iraqi *Untermenschen* who have died in such grotesque numbers over the past two decades. But when the perpetrator of mass-atrocity crimes is our enemy or a state targeted by us for destabilization and attack, the converse is true. Then the atrocities are nefarious and their victims worthy of our focus, sympathy, public displays of solidarity, and calls for inquiry and punishment. Nefarious atrocities even have their own proper names reserved for them, typically associated with the places where the events occur. We can all rattle off the most notorious: Cambodia (but only under the Khmer Rouge, not in the prior years of mass killing by the United States and its allies), Iraq (but only when attributable to Saddam Hussein, not the United States), and so on—Halabja, Bosnia, Srebrenica, Rwanda, Kosovo, Raak, Darfur. Indeed, receiving such a baptism is perhaps the hallmark of the nefarious bloodbath."

Justifying U.S. Acts of Genocide

To reiterate their point: When the killing, maiming, poisoning and displacement of millions of civilians are perpetrated by the U.S. directly and in collusion with a client regime it assists, arms and advises—Indochina in the 1960s and early 1970s, Central America in the 1980s, the deaths of as many as a million Iraqis resulting from sanctions and the deliberate and systematic destruction of civilian infrastructure in the 1990s—that form of indisputable genocide is never referred to as such and instead presented by the government-media-obedient academia triad as not abhorrent and criminal but as legitimate actions in pursuit of praiseworthy policies. Constructive genocide.

Similar systematic and large-scale atrocities carried out by U.S. clients armed by Washington—Indonesia against its own people from 1965–1966 and in East Timor from 1975–1999, Israel in the Palestinian Gaza Strip and West Bank from 1967 to the present day, Rwanda and Uganda in the Congo (where over five and a half million people have perished over the last twelve years), Croatia and its Operation Storm onslaught in 1995 which caused the worst permanent ethnic cleansing in Europe since World War II and its immediate aftermath—are not condemned and not even deemed regrettable, but in fact are viewed by the U.S. political establishment as benign.

Contrariwise, though, security and military actions taken by governments not aligned with the U.S., even against armed and cross-border separatist formations, are inevitably branded as gratuitous acts of what Samuel Coleridge called motiveless malignancy: nefarious genocide.

Related to the last category, the U.S. government and its news and NGO [nongovernmental organization] camp followers are not averse to inflating numbers, misattributing the cause of death and outright inventing incidents to justify the charge of genocide and what are frequently pre-planned interventions, including sanctions, embargoes, travel bans on government officials, freezing governments' financial assets abroad, funding and advising assorted "color revolutions" and ultimately bombing from 25,000 feet, beyond the range of a targeted country's air defenses. What the authors call mythic genocide, though with quite genuine—deadly—consequences. Aesop: The boys throw rocks in jest but the frogs die in earnest.

Media Examples

To illustrate these basic categories, Herman and Peterson conducted exhaustive database searches for usage of the word "genocide" by some of the major English-language print media in reference to what they call "theaters of atrocities."

The three tables they have compiled for the book are something to behold.

Table 1 is titled "Differential attributions of 'genocide' to different theaters of atrocities," and Table [3] "Differential Use of 'Massacre' and 'Genocide' for Benign and Nefarious Atrocities;" Table 2 focuses on different aspects of Iraq specifically.

The various "theaters of atrocities" include but are not limited to Iraq, the Muslims of Bosnia-Herzegovina, the ethnic Albanians of Kosovo, the Tutsi of Rwanda, the Hutu and other peoples of the Democratic Republic of the Congo, and the peoples of western Sudan (Darfur).

In one of the more impressive empirical confirmations of a hypothesis readers are likely to find anywhere, the results of Herman and Peterson's database research are both predictable and appalling: In case after case, major English-language newspapers such as the *New York Times* and the *Guardian* (as well as countless others) used the word "genocide" in a manner that would have been approved of by the State Department, linking it consistently to toponyms like Rwanda, Bosnia, Kosovo and Darfur, but rarely if ever to the Democratic Republic of the Congo, Palestine, Afghanistan, and Iraq, whether Iraq during the "sanctions of mass destruction" era (1990–2003) or since the U.S. invasion and military occupation (from 2003 onward).

Worthy vs. Unworthy Victims

There are, in the terms introduced by Edward [S.] Herman and Noam Chomsky years earlier, "worthy" and "unworthy" victims in the system of "atrocities management," and each and every victim's worthiness rises or falls depending on who's doing the killing—official enemies or we ourselves.

Again, to elaborate: The worthiness of a victim to elicit concern and support depends not on the victim himself but on the "worthiness" of the perpetrator. "Good" perpetrators—the U.S. and its allies—are eo ipso [by that fact alone] incapable of bad actions, therefore anyone on the receiving end of an American bomb or cruise missile is inherently unworthy.

Genocide, murder on a grand scale, is treated not with the urgency and gravity the subject warrants but as the theme of a near–comic book morality play. We and they, good and bad.

An analogous bias exists, the authors detail, in relation to the work of the International Criminal Court and even more so with the International Criminal Tribunal for the former Yugoslavia and the International Criminal Tribunal for Rwanda.

The latter two are nothing other than the embodiment and institutionalization of great power victor's justice and the first is used by the U.S. against recalcitrant states on Washington's enemies list. (In the foreword to *The Politics of Genocide*, Chomsky cites the Greek historian Thucydides, who placed in the mouth of an Athenian the immortal words: "you know as well as we do that right, as the world goes, is only in question between equals in power, while the strong do what they can and the weak suffer what they must.")

The Nuremberg Principles

International courts doing the bidding of the U.S. and its North Atlantic Treaty Organization [NATO] cohorts do not, Herman and Peterson point out, address the greatest cause of suffering brought about through human agency: wars of aggression. Although borrowing their lexicon from the Nuremberg principles—for example, "war crimes" and "crimes of humanity"—while adding "genocide" and "ethnic cleansing" (with the last two used all but interchangeably), Western states are highly selective and equally self-serving in their interpretation of the Nuremberg tribunal, the model for prosecuting international crimes of violence.

Principle VI, the gist of the Nuremberg indictments, states:

The crimes hereinafter set out are punishable as crimes under international law:

> (a) Crimes against peace:
>
> > 1. (i) Planning, preparation, initiation or waging of a war of aggression or a war in violation of international treaties, agreements or assurances;
> >
> > 2. (ii) Participation in a common plan or conspiracy for the accomplishment of any of the acts mentioned under (i).
>
> (b) War crimes:
>
> Violations of the laws or customs of war which include, but are not limited to, murder, ill-treatment or deportation of slave labor or for any other purpose of the civilian population of or in occupied territory; murder or ill-treatment of prisoners of war or persons on the Seas, killing of hostages, plunder of public or private property, wanton destruction of cities, towns, or villages, or devastation not justified by military necessity.
>
> (c) Crimes against humanity:
>
> Murder, extermination, enslavement, deportation and other inhumane acts done against any civilian population, or persecutions on political, racial, or religious grounds, when such acts are done or such persecutions are carried on in execution of or in connection with any crime against peace or any war crime.

Wars of Aggression

The U.S. and its Western allies, which launched three wars of aggression in less than four years (Yugoslavia in 1999, Afghanistan in 2001 and Iraq in 2003) with the forced displacement of millions of civilians, have deliberately chosen to ignore the core proscription of the Nuremberg trials, that against waging wars of aggression, "the supreme international crime, differing only from other war crimes in that it contains within itself the accumulated evil of the whole."

Principle VII says that "Complicity in the commission of a crime against peace, a war crime, or a crime against humanity as set forth in Principle VI is a crime under international law."

Selective Enforcement

To relentlessly prosecute lesser crimes while perpetrating and abetting greater ones is the prerogative of the "world's sole military superpower" (from Barack Obama's Nobel Peace Prize acceptance speech) and its allies. Governments of small, weak countries not sufficiently toeing Washington's line are threatened with prosecution for actions occurring within and not outside their borders and the only "war crimes" trials conducted are also exclusively in response to strictly internal events. By design and selective enforcement, the new system of international law is what [Honoré] Balzac said of the law of his time, that it is a spider web through which the big flies pass and the little ones get caught.

Herman and Peterson have studied the above contrasts, what most often are an inversion of justice and not simply its distortion or selective implementation, in several locations: the Balkans, the Middle East, Southeast Asia and Latin America, examining the most salient examples in each locale to demonstrate the unconscionable dichotomy of "good" and bad genocides.

In one of the most penetrating sections of the book, the authors study the differential approach of the U.S. in the contexts of both space and time; that is, how the suppression of the Kurdish movement has been treated in relation to Iraq as opposed to Turkey, and in Iraq from one decade to the next depending on whether the same head of state (Saddam Hussein) was a U.S. ally or adversary at the time.

Not a matter of what is right or wrong, not even of who does what to whom, but solely one of what advances America's narrow and cynical geopolitical agenda.

Their model, however, possesses relevance to developments in other nations beyond those studied in *The Politics of Genocide*. Colombia, for example, and western Sahara.

Also to Kosovo after 50,000 U.S. and NATO troops marched in eleven years ago and hundreds of thousands of Serbs, Roma (Gypsies) and other ethnic minorities were forced to flee the Serbian province.

Benign Attempts of Genocide

Onslaughts against the people of South Ossetia two years ago this August [2010] by preeminent U.S. client Mikheil Saakashvili in Georgia and against the Houthi minority community in northern Yemen with military backing from Saudi Arabia and the U.S. would be examples of benign attempts to exterminate entire peoples, to commit genocide.

During the generation following the end of the Cold War and the triumph of global neoliberalism, enough genuine problems have weighed upon humanity. With the privatization of increasingly broad sectors of former state functions and the concomitant economic dislocation of a large percentage of the population, and with the penetration of rapacious transnational financial and corporate interests, tens of millions—perhaps hundreds of millions—of people in poor countries have fled the countryside to the large cities. Millions more have attempted the desperate and often deadly migration to the global North. The last twenty years have witnessed the largest *Völkerwanderung* [migration of people] in history.

In that context, competition for natural and other resources takes on a drastic intensity, and conflicts based on residual ethnic, religious and regional suspicions and strife can be too easily revived and inflamed. The potential for communal, for interethnic, violence is a power keg that must not be ignited.

The willful exacerbation and exploitation of such conflicts by outside powers to achieve broader geostrategic objectives add a greater degree of peril, one of regional conflicts that could expand into wider wars and even a showdown between the U.S. and nuclear powers like Russia and China.

The U.S. government and its highly selective "genocide" echo chambers are adept at seeing the mote in their neighbor's eye, but are blind to the mountain of corpses produced by Washington and its proxies.

Exploiting Tragedy

The 78-day bombing war waged by the U.S. and NATO against Yugoslavia in 1999 in the name of "stopping genocide," the "worst genocide since Hitler," coincided with the induction of the first former Warsaw Pact member states into the Alliance (the Czech Republic, Hungary and Poland) and resulted in the building of a mammoth U.S. military base, Camp Bondsteel, in Kosovo and NATO's absorption and penetration of all of southeastern Europe. Every country in the region but Serbia (for the time being) now has troops serving under the military bloc in Afghanistan.

The crisis in Darfur in western Sudan gave rise to NATO's first operation in Africa, the airlifting of African Union troops from 2005–2007. At the end of 2007 the first U.S. military command established outside North America since the Cold War, [U.S.] Africa Command, was launched.

In the same year and in the name of opposing genocide, a self-styled "March for Darfur" was held in Berkeley, California—a birthplace of the anti–Vietnam War protest movement forty years before—in which participants adapted a standard anti-war chant—"What do we want? Peace! When do we want it? Now!"—to "What do we want? NATO! When do we want it? Now!"

Ending Genocide?

At the end of the day, military actions, including full-fledged wars, conducted by the U.S. and NATO in part or in whole to ostensibly "end genocide" will produce more deaths, more mass-scale displacement, and more expulsion and extermination of endangered minorities as has happened over the past eleven years in Kosovo, Iraq and Afghanistan. More genocide. The genuine article.

Questions about the intentional and systematic extermination of a people are not to be taken lightly. Neither are they to be dealt with as yet another weapon in the arsenal of history's mightiest military power for use against defenseless adversaries. The U.S. government and its highly selective "genocide" echo chambers are adept at seeing the mote in their neighbor's eye, but are blind to the mountain of corpses produced by Washington and its proxies. Myopia passing into active complicity.

In documenting the diametrically opposite manner in which the subject of genocide is treated by the government of the United States and its apologists (acknowledged and otherwise) based on international political and economic motives, Herman and Peterson have provided a simultaneously concise and comprehensive guidebook to separating fact from fabrication. Truth is the first casualty of war and war is in turn the offspring of falsehood. Exposing the last contributes to eroding the foundation for U.S. armed aggression and global military expansion.

Israel Should Encourage a Greater Understanding of the Universality of Genocide

Benyamin Neuberger

Benyamin Neuberger is a professor of political science at the Open University. In the following viewpoint, he rejects the Israeli conviction that the Holocaust is unique and cannot be compared to any other genocide. Neuberger considers it essential to teach Israeli schoolchildren about other genocides, including the horrors of the Rwandan genocide of 1994, because it instills a respect for people and human life and shows Israelis that they are bonded to people of other nations. Comparing recent genocides to the Holocaust does not demean the suffering of the Jewish people; it teaches universal lessons of the value of human life, Neuberger maintains, and the importance of fighting intolerance, injustice, and ignorance.

As you read, consider the following questions:

1. According to the author, how many people in Rwanda were murdered in a span of three months during the 1994 genocide?
2. How many Tutsis does the author say were murdered in a Nyanga church in April 1994?
3. What did the author find in Kigali?

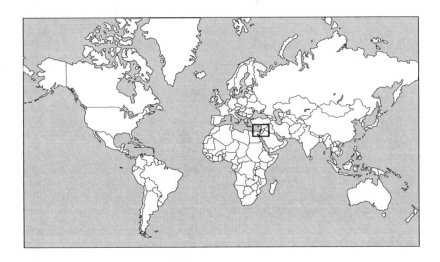

In Israel, there is a conviction that the Holocaust is unique, that it cannot be compared to any other case of genocide. This perception is irrational, problematic from the moral perspective and also contrary to its aim—the intensification of Holocaust awareness.

The Rwandan Genocide

I have just returned from Rwanda, where the genocide of the Tutsi people was carried out a dozen years ago—about 1 million people were murdered in three months. I stood at the Murumbi site and I learned that in this place, 54,000 Tutsi were murdered in cold blood. There are only four known survivors. One of them stood there before me and told me about babies who were flung live into pits, which were covered with dirt. I saw skeletons, and clothes taken from those who were murdered. I could not help but recall my visit to the Nazi death camps in Poland. However, we have been taught that it is forbidden to compare.

In Nyanga, I visited the ruins of a church into which, in those terrible days of April 1994, 2,000 Tutsi were forced. They were abandoned by a Hutu priest, who handed them over to the Interahamwe militia, who murdered all of them.

Again I recalled synagogues that were set on fire by the Nazis, with their Jews inside, but I had to fight this memory, because after all, it is forbidden to compare.

Teaching of the Holocaust in a way that presents only Jewish uniqueness leads to a conviction that the Jewish people will always dwell alone . . . and therefore universal morality and international law are of no importance.

The time has come to say that the approach that negates comparison does not stand the test of reason. After all, anyone who says that it is forbidden to compare says this after he has made the comparison. Comparison does not mean that everything is identical—but rather that there is a similarity, and there could also be a difference. There is no contradiction between comparing the Holocaust to other cases of genocide and the statement that the Holocaust is the largest genocide.

A Lost Cause

The fight to isolate the Holocaust and disconnect it from the slaughter of other peoples is in any case a lost cause. More and more books are being published that deal with comparisons. Recently, the International Association of Genocide Scholars was founded, and the foremost researchers at universities in America and Europe are members.

The approach that the Holocaust must not be compared to other genocides has meant that a high school student in Israel knows nothing about the genocide of the Armenian people, the genocide in Rwanda or even the slaughter of the Roma, or Gypsies, during World War II. Teaching of the Holocaust in a way that presents only Jewish uniqueness leads to a conviction that the Jewish people will always dwell alone, that gentiles must not be considered, that all of them are Amalek [Biblical enemies of the Hebrews], and therefore universal morality and international law are of no importance.

The Rwanda Genocide

Three African ethnic groups inhabit Rwanda: the Tutsi, the Hutu, and the tiny population of the Twa. These groups co-existed for centuries. Tutsis held the highest social status, but a Hutu could advance to the status of a Tutsi. The general population intermarried and lived in ethnically mixed communities. The two groups fought in the same army and shared the same religion, language, and political culture. . . .

On 6 April 1994, as [Rwandan President Juvénal] Habyarimana flew to Dar es Salaam, Tanzania, for a round of peace talks, his plane was shot down. Habyarimana and the president of Burundi were both killed. No one knew who was behind the killing, but the assassination inflamed Rwanda's extremist Hutus, who immediately sent out an order for Rwanda's mayors, militias, and death squads to start killing the Tutsis.

The genocide began with the assassination of every Tutsi in the cabinet. Death lists were established and everyone on them was hunted down and killed. The Interahamwe (those who attack together), an unofficial militia group of about 30,000 fighters, was organized. . . . Hutu gangs armed with swords, spears, and machetes attacked Tutsis, hacking, clubbing, or beating them to death.

The Tutsis fled, gathering in central locations, such as hospitals, churches, and stadiums. . . . Hutu militias threw hand grenades into the buildings housing the Tutsis. Anyone who ran out was shot and Tutsis remaining alive inside were hacked to death. Many who survived the initial killings were raped and mutilated. An estimated twenty thousand people died per day during the slaughter.

"Rwanda Genocide," Global Issues in Context Online, *2011.*

A number of years ago I participated in a conference at Bar-Ilan University that was devoted to a discussion of the trips to Poland undertaken by Israeli teenagers. The woman responsible for the trips at the Ministry of Education spoke about their aim—strengthening the high school students' Jewish identity and Zionist consciousness. In answer to the question of whether the trips have a humanistic aim as well, an outrageous answer was given: "We don't have time for that."

The Lessons of Rwanda

We should instill awareness of the Holocaust that leads to conclusions about the need for a Jewish state and an army, but also universal lessons about respect for every human being and every people and opposition to all discrimination, racism and oppression. Such an awareness can be instilled by means of teaching the Holocaust alongside the study of other cases of genocide.

On this issue we can in fact learn from Rwanda. When they talk about the lesson of "never again" they stress "never again genocide" of any people anywhere. In contrast to us, who do not know anything about the genocide in Rwanda, they know a great deal about the Jewish Holocaust. And at their Yad Vashem [memorial to victims], in their capital, Kigali, there is a corner that deals with the Holocaust, the genocide of the Cambodian people and other cases of genocide.

England Should Recognize the Armenian Genocide

Vahe Gabrielyan

Vahe Gabrielyan is the Armenian ambassador to England. In the following viewpoint, he contends that it is vital for Turkey to admit to and apologize for perpetrating a genocide of the Armenian people that resulted in the deaths of millions of Armenian Christians. Years ago the international community acknowledged the genocide of 1915, but today criticism of Turkey is muted for political reasons, Gabrielyan maintains. Turkish denial of the genocide effectively ends any chance of reconciliation between Armenia and Turkey. The British government can affirm its stated values of human rights and democracy by publicly urging Turkey to do the right thing, the author concludes.

As you read, consider the following questions:

1. According to Gabrielyan, how long did the Armenian genocide last?
2. What does the author say that Winston Churchill called the 1915 massacre of Armenians?
3. As of 2007, how many British MPs signed an Early Day Motion to raise awareness about the Armenian genocide?

Vahe Gabrielyan, "Time to Recognise the Armenian Genocide," *New Statesman*, October 12, 2007. www.newstatesman.com. Copyright © 2007 by New Statesman. All rights reserved. Reproduced by permission.

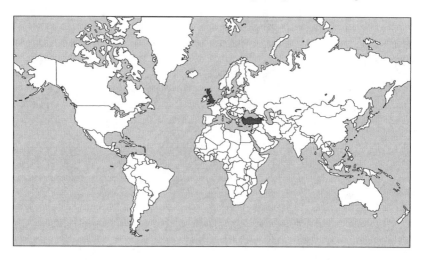

Throughout the twentieth century to the present day there has not been any substantiated doubt about the character of the mass deportations, expropriation, abduction, torture, starvation and killings of millions of Armenians throughout Ottoman Turkey that started on a large scale in 1915 and carried on to 1923.

Centrally planned by the government of the day and meticulously executed by the huge machine of the state bureaucracy, army, police, hired gangs and—specially released for that purpose—criminals from prisons, the campaign had one clear aim expressly stated by the government in secret directives: to rid Anatolia of its indigenous Armenian population and settle the so-called "Armenian question" for good.

Defining the Genocide

An entire nation and its Christian culture were eliminated to secure a homogenous Turkish state on territories where Armenians had lived for many centuries.

Terms such as "genocide" or "ethnic cleansing" were not in circulation then, so Winston Churchill later referred to the 1915 massacre of 1.5 million Armenians as an "administrative holocaust".

47

The Turkish authorities made no secret of the aim once it was achieved and other governments and nations have known the truth since. One of the early accounts of Armenian genocide was published in 1916 in Britain.

The British government at the time commissioned James Bryce and Arnold Toynbee to compile evidence on the events in Armenia. The subsequent report was printed in the British Parliamentary Blue Book series *The Treatment of Armenians in the Ottoman Empire, 1915–1916.* The report leaves no doubt about what was taking place.

In 1915, thirty-three years before the UN [United Nations] genocide convention was adopted, the Armenian genocide was condemned by the international community as a crime against humanity. It is well acknowledged that Polish jurist Raphael Lemkin, when he coined the term genocide in 1944, cited the Turkish extermination of the Armenians and the Nazi extermination of the Jews as defining examples of what he meant by genocide.

Armenians throughout the world insist that there be an international recognition and condemnation of what is often called the first genocide of the twentieth century.

Silencing the Truth

Amidst huge international pressure, the Turkish government succeeding the Young Turks had not only to recognise the scale and vehemence of the atrocities but also to try the perpetrators in military tribunals and sentence the leaders to death.

However, the sentences were not carried out and with the passage of time moods changed not only in Turkey but also in some countries, such as the UK [United Kingdom], where Turkey is nowadays seen as a key ally. Still, even in countries that have not yet for some reason recognised the genocide, scholars have no doubts about the character of the events: They point out that there is no scholarly issue, only one of political expediency.

Demands for Recognition

Armenians throughout the world insist that there be an international recognition and condemnation of what is often called the first genocide of the twentieth century. We are past the stage of scholarly discussion since a very few challenge the fact. To dispel any doubt, 126 leading scholars of the Holocaust placed a statement in the *New York Times* in June 2000 declaring the "incontestable fact of the Armenian Genocide" and urging Western democracies to acknowledge it.

In 2005 the International Association of Genocide Scholars addressed an open letter to Turkey's Prime Minister [Recep Tayyip] Erdogan calling upon him to recognise the truth. The evidence is so overwhelming that the only question remaining is how to help the two nations close that shameful page of the history, reconcile and move forward.

However, despite the affirmation of the Armenian genocide by the overwhelming majority of historians, academic institutions on Holocaust and Genocide Studies, increasingly more parliaments and governments around the world, and by more and more Turkish scholars and intellectuals, the Turkish government still actively denies the fact. So long as they do that, Armenians have no choice but to struggle for wider international recognition.

Turkey Must Take Responsibility

This is however not an end in itself. It is important that Turkey recognises the genocide, apologizes and condemns it. When the Germans have apologized for the sufferings they had caused to the Jews, the British for slavery, the Americans for their treatment of Native Americans, etc., Turkey's continuing denial, moreover, increasing efforts and resources

The Assassination of Hrant Dink

Hrant Dink worked since 1996 as a columnist and editor in chief of the Armenian-language weekly newspaper *Agos* in Istanbul. The paper aims to provide a voice for the Armenian community in Turkey and to further dialogue between Turks and Armenians.

On 19 January 2007, Hrant Dink was assassinated outside *Agos*'s offices in Istanbul.

"Hrant Dink (1954–2007): In Memoriam,"
openDemocracy, January 22, 2007. www.opendemocracy.net.

spent on the denial are alarming signs, aggravated by their insistence not to establish diplomatic relations with neighbouring Armenia and by maintaining a blockade on all ground communication. Armenia does not even set the recognition of the genocide as a prerequisite for normalizing relations and calls for establishing diplomatic relations and opening of the border without any preconditions.

As the killing this January [2007] of Hrant Dink, the Turkish-Armenian editor of the *Agos* bilingual periodical demonstrates, the international community cannot stand aside and watch. Hrant was persecuted under the infamous 301 article for "insulting Turkish identity" and the hysteria around someone daring to speak the truth created the fertile soil for the hatred that killed him. His case was shamefully still open even after his assassination and in a demonstration of absolute absence of morality, Turkish courts yesterday [in October 2007] sentenced Hrant's son, as well as another of *Agos*'s current staff, to a year of imprisonment under the same accusations, for simply daring to reprint Hrant's words.

Rejecting Blackmail

This is why the world should not yield to Turkish threats that are outright blackmailing. The resolutions in various legislatures across the world, and recently in the US House of Representative Foreign [Affairs] Committee, are not merely the result of Armenian Diaspora's—which by the way, was created in the first place because of the genocide in Turkey—influence. It is because there are more people who believe in values and in putting the wrongs right.

A number of British MPs [members of Parliament] have tabled an EDM (Early Day Motion), to raise the awareness about the Armenian genocide and calling on British government to recognise it as such. Currently, around 170 MPs across the party lines have signed an EDM which reads "That this House believes that the killing of over a million Armenians in 1915 was an act of genocide; calls upon the UK Government to recognise it as such; and believes that it would be in Turkey's long-term interests to do the same."

Their number grows steadily. It is time the British government followed many others and reaffirmed the UK's place among the standard-bearers of democracy and human rights.

It is worth repeating that international recognition of the genocide cannot do harm to Turkish-Armenian relations since they simply do not exist. It does not prevent a dialogue, on the contrary, creates the necessary conditions to start a frank one. By recognising the historic truth and helping open the last closed border in Europe, the international community can facilitate long-lasting stability and prosperity in our region. And it is also probably time to show that the human race's evolution into the 21st century is evolution of ideals, principles and a code of behaviour that should take precedence over political expediency or sheer commercial interest.

Germany Has Not Recognized Armenian Genocide Because of the Political Implications

Benjamin Bidder, Daniel Steinvorth, and Bernhard Zand

Benjamin Bidder, Daniel Steinvorth, and Bernhard Zand are journalists. In the following viewpoint, they describe a 2010 German documentary that presents firsthand accounts from witnesses to the Armenian genocide as a powerful reminder of the horror and brutality of the massacre. The authors observe that although Germany has urged Turkey to acknowledge its historical responsibility, it has avoided using the word "genocide" in order to placate an important ally. Increasing pressure on the Turkish government and dissent from Armenians in Turkey has led to violence and tension, the authors explain.

As you read, consider the following questions:

1. How many people do the authors say were killed during the Armenian genocide?

2. According to the authors, what has Turkish prime minister Recep Tayyip Erdogan said about the Armenian genocide?

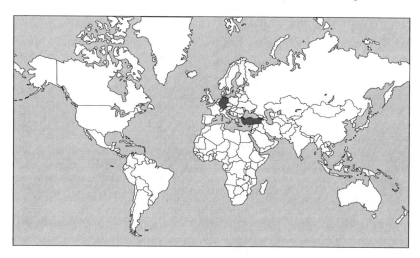

3. When did the Committee on Foreign Affairs of the US House of Representatives pass a resolution to acknowledge the Armenian genocide?

Tigranui Asartyan will be 100 this week [in April 2010]. She put away her knives and forks two years ago, when she lost her sense of taste, and last year she stopped wearing glasses, having lost her sight. She lives on the seventh floor of a high-rise building in the Armenian capital Yerevan, and she hasn't left her room in months. She shivers as the cold penetrates the gray wool blanket on her lap. "I'm waiting to die," she says.

Ninety-two years ago, she was waiting in a village on the Turkish side of today's border, hiding in the cellar of a house. The body of an Armenian boy who had been beaten to death lay on the street. Women were being raped in the house next door, and the eight-year-old girl could hear them screaming. "There are good and bad Turks," she says. The bad Turks beat the boy to death, while the good Turks helped her and her family to flee behind withdrawing Russian troops.

Avadis Demirci, a farmer, is 97. If anyone in his country keeps records on such things, he is probably the last Armenian in Turkey who survived the genocide. Demirci looks out the window at the village of Vakifli, where oleander bushes and tangerine trees are in full bloom. The Mediterranean is visible down the mountain and in the distance.

In July 1915, Turkish police units marched up to the village. "My father strapped me to his back when we fled," says Demirci. "At least that's what my parents told me." Armed with hunting rifles and pistols, the people from his and six other villages dug themselves in on Musa Dagh, or Moses Mountain. Eighteen years later, Austrian writer Franz Werfel described the villagers' armed resistance against the advancing soldiers in his novel *The Forty Days of Musa Dagh*.

"The story is true," says Demirci. "I experienced it, even if I am only familiar with it from the stories I was told."

The Armenian people, after suffering partial annihilation, then being scattered around the world and forced back to a country that has remained isolated to this day, have taken decades to come to terms with their own catastrophe.

Avoiding the Word

Aside from Werfel's book—and the view, from the memorial on Tsitsernakaberd hill near Yerevan, of the eternally snow-capped and eternally inaccessible Mount Ararat—there are few reminders left of the Armenian genocide as its last few survivors approach death.

Between 1915 and 1918, some 800,000 to 1.5 million people were murdered in what is now eastern Turkey, or died on death marches in the northern Syrian desert. It was one of the first genocides of the 20th century. Other genocides—against the European Jews, in Cambodia and in Rwanda—have since taken their place in history between the Armenian genocide and today.

The Armenian people, after suffering partial annihilation, then being scattered around the world and forced back to a country that has remained isolated to this day, have taken decades to come to terms with their own catastrophe. It was only in the 1960s, after a long debate with the leadership in Moscow, that the Armenians dared to erect a memorial.

Turkey, on whose territory the crimes were committed, continues to deny the actions of the Ottoman leadership. Germany, allied with the Ottoman Empire in World War I, and the Soviet Union, well-disposed toward the young Turkish republic, had no interest in publicizing the genocide.

Germany has still not officially recognized the Armenian genocide. In 2005, the German parliament, the Bundestag, called upon Turkey to acknowledge its "historical responsibility," but it avoided using word "genocide."

Because of Ankara's [the capital of Turkey] political and strategic importance in the Cold War, its Western allies did not view a debate over the genocide as opportune. And the relative lack of photographic and film material—compared with the Holocaust and later genocides—has made it even more difficult to examine and come to terms with the Armenian catastrophe. "The development of modern media," says German documentary filmmaker Eric Friedler (*The Silence of the Quandts*), "arrived 20 years too late for the examination of this genocide."

But there are contemporary witnesses, Germans and Americans, in particular, whose accounts and correspondence are preserved in archives, where they have been studied mainly by specialists until now. This Friday, to mark the 95th anniversary of the genocide, Germany's ARD television network will air the elaborately researched documentary *Aghet* (Armenian for "Catastrophe"), which brings the words of diplomats, engineers and missionaries to life.

An ensemble of 23 German actors narrates the original texts—not in the style of a docu-drama, which re-enacts the events using semi-fictional dialogue and historic costumers, but in simple interviews that derive their effectiveness from the selection of texts and the presentation rather than a dramatization of history.

Firsthand Documents

The first performer is actor and author Hanns Zischler, who starred in director Wim Wenders' 1976 film *Im Lauf der Zeit* (or *Kings of the Road*). He reads the words of Leslie Davis, who, until 1917, was the US consul in the eastern Anatolian city of Harput, where thousands of Armenians were herded together and sent on a death march toward the southeast. "On Saturday, June 28th," Davis wrote, "it was publicly announced that all Armenians and Syrians [Assyrians of the Armenian Apostolic faith] were to leave after five days. The full meaning of such an order can scarcely be imagined by those who are not familiar with the peculiar conditions of this isolated region. A massacre, however horrible the word may sound, would be humane in comparison with it."

Friedrich von Thun, a film and television actor who appeared in Steven Spielberg's film *Schindler's List*, plays US Ambassador Henry Morgenthau. He describes encounters with Ottoman Interior Minister Talaat Pasha, who, at the beginning of the operation, confronted Morgenthau with the "irrevocable decision" to render the Armenians "harmless."

After the genocide, Talaat summoned the US ambassador again and made a request that Morgenthau said was "perhaps the most astonishing thing I had ever heard." Talaat wanted the lists of Armenian customers of the American insurance companies New York Life Insurance and Equitable Life. The Armenians were now dead and had no heirs, he said, and the government was therefore entitled to their benefits. "Naturally, I turned down his request," Morgenthau wrote.

Actresses Martina Gedeck and Katharina Schüttler recount the memories of two missionary sisters, one Swedish and the other Swiss. Hannah Herzsprung and Ludwig Trepte narrate the experiences of two survivors, and Peter Lohmeyer reads from the diary of German Consul Wilhelm Litten, one of the most shocking documents of the time.

On Jan. 31, 1916, Litten was on the road between Deir al-Zor and Tibni in present-day Syria, where he wrote the following entry into his diary: "One o'clock in the afternoon. On the left side of the road is a young woman, naked, wearing only brown stockings on her feet, her back turned upward and her head buried in her crossed arms. 1:30 p.m. In a ditch on the right side is an old man with a white beard, naked, lying on his back. Two steps away is a boy, naked, back turned upward, his left buttock ripped off."

Equally cold and calculating was the reply of then chancellor of the German Reich, Theobald von Bethmann-Hollweg, to the German ambassador's proposal to publicly rebuke Germany's Ottoman allies for the crime. "Our only goal was to keep Turkey on our side until the end of the war, regardless of whether or not Armenians perished."

Turkey's Denial of Its Wrongs

The wealth of image and film documents gathered from archives as distant as Moscow and Washington [DC], says author and director Friedler, even surprised the historians who provided him with expert advice for his 90-minute film. Some incidents, such as the ostentatious 1943 reburial in Turkey of the remains of Talaat Pasha, who was murdered in Berlin in 1921, will be shown on film for the first time. Other documents depict individuals who the archivists had not recognized there before.

The film also offers an oppressive description of the current debate over the genocide, which is only now erupting in Turkey, almost a century after the crime. Prime Minister Recep Tayyip Erdogan blusters that Turkey will never admit that genocide took place. During an exhibition on Armenia, ultra-

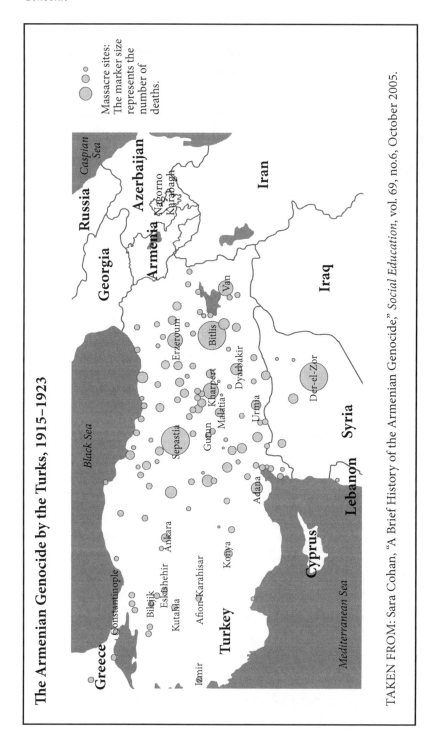

The Armenian Genocide by the Turks, 1915–1923

Massacre sites:
The marker size represents the number of deaths.

TAKEN FROM: Sara Cohan, "A Brief History of the Armenian Genocide," *Social Education*, vol. 69, no.6, October 2005.

nationalists angrily rip photographs from the walls, and then, as if they've lost their minds, they attack a car in which Orhan Pamuk, winner of the Nobel Prize for literature, is being taken home after a court appearance—because he dared to express what historians had proven long ago.

The demons of the past are now awakening in response to pressure, particularly from the Armenian Diaspora.

For decades, Armenians born after the genocide felt tortured and troubled by it. "The tragedy," says Hayk Demoyan, the director of the genocide memorial in Yerevan, has become "a pillar of our national identity." And Armenian President Serge Sarkisian has told *SPIEGEL*: "The best way to prevent the repetition of such an atrocity is to condemn it clearly."

The post-genocide generation of Turks had no trouble sleeping. Mustafa Kemal Atatürk, the founder of the Turkish republic, made a radical break with the Ottoman Empire and the three men who were primarily responsible—Talaat, Enver and Cemal Pasha. Atatürk admitted that "wrongs" had been committed, wrongs his successors deny to this day, but he also let government officials and military leaders participate in his government who had been directly involved in the genocide.

A Living, Hidden Memory

The demons of the past are now awakening in response to pressure, particularly from the Armenian Diaspora. Every spring, before the April 24 anniversary of the arrests of Armenian politicians and intellectuals in what was then Constantinople, arrests that marked the beginning of the deportations in 1915, more national parliaments adopt resolutions to acknowledge the Armenian genocide: France in 2001, Switzerland in 2003 and, this year [2010], the Foreign Affairs Committee of the US House of Representatives and the Swedish parliament.

Every time one of these resolutions is passed, Ankara threatens with political consequences—and ultimately never follows through. It has become a ritual, the purpose of which men like Hrant Dink have questioned. The publisher of the Turkish-Armenia newspaper *Agos* didn't dwell on the definition of the word "genocide." Instead, he wanted Turkey to confront its gruesome past directly.

He paid for his views with his life. On Jan. 19, 2007, Dink was murdered in broad daylight. The 200,000 Turks who marched through the streets of Istanbul at his funeral, holding up banners that read "We are all Armenians," humiliated their own government with their forthrightness. A reality which thousands of Turks are confronted with in their own families appears to have had a stronger impact than diplomatic pressure.

In the early 1980s, Istanbul attorney Fethiye Çetin discovered that she had Armenian roots. Her grandmother Seher had confided in her after several anguishing decades. In 1915 Seher, who was baptized with the Armenian name Heranush, witnessed the throats of men in her village being slit. She survived, was taken in by the family of a Turkish officer, was raised as a Muslim girl and eventually married a Turk. She became one of tens of thousands of "hidden Armenians" who escaped the murderers and blended in with Turkish society.

Her grandmother's revelation came as a shock to Çetin, and she began to see her surroundings with different eyes. In 2004, Çetin wrote a book in which she outlined the history of her family. *Anneannem* (*My Grandmother*) became a best seller, and countless readers contacted Çetin, many with words of appreciation.

Others cursed her as a "traitor." But the taboo had been broken.

Turkey's Denial of Armenian Genocide Is Holding It Back

Colin Tatz

Colin Tatz is a visiting fellow in the College of Arts & Social Sciences at the Australian National University and is the author of With Intent to Destroy: Reflecting on Genocide. *In the following viewpoint, he maintains that Turkey's obsessive and hysterical denial of its role in the Armenian genocide defies rational explanation and hinders its relationship with the European Union. Tatz argues the denial industry in Turkey has grown so strong and defiant that there is little hope that the country can come to terms with its history. He also predicts that Australia will one day soon pass a resolution to acknowledge the Armenian genocide, as several regional governments have already done.*

As you read, consider the following questions:

1. How many nation-states does Tatz say have formally acknowledged the Armenian genocide?
2. How does the author say Turkey explains the charges against it?
3. According to the author, how many Armenians died in 1915 "at the hands of the Young Turks"?

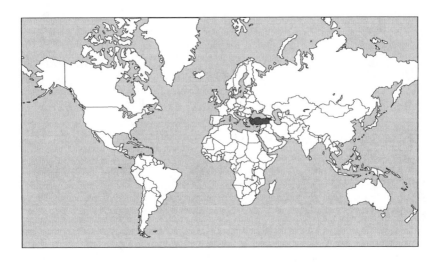

The idea that Australia was born as a nation on Gallipoli's shores [the Battle of Gallipoli was a key World War I battle in Turkey] is now deeply cemented in our history books and national psyche. We are about to see the annual holding of hands by the former combatants on Armistice Day, when thousands will visit the "sacred site". Turks and Australians will join in understandable commemoration but less comprehensible celebration; and friendship societies will become tearful and lyrical during this anniversary of the shedding of brotherly blood.

But intruding on this mourning ritual is the growing world recognition of the Ottoman (and, later, Kemalist) Turkish genocide committed between 1915 and 1923. Some 26 nation-states and more than 50 regional governments, including NSW [New South Wales] and South Australia, formally recognise the Turkish attempts to annihilate 3 million Armenians and possibly 1 million Pontian Greeks and Christian Assyrians. At least 1.5 million Armenians were killed by bayoneting, beheading, bullets, butchering, crucifixion, drowning, elementary gas chambers, forced death marches, hanging, hot horseshoes, medical experiments, and other unprintable atrocities.

The Denial Industry in Turkey

Turkey is totally dedicated, at home and abroad, to having every hint or mention of an Armenian genocide contradicted, countered, explained, justified, mitigated, rationalised, relativised, removed or trivialised. The entire apparatus of the Turkish state is tuned to denial, with officers appointed abroad for that purpose. Their actions are spectacular, often bizarre, and without distinction between the serious and the silly, including: pressures to dilute or even remove any mention of the genocide in the Armenian entry in the *Encyclopaedia Britannica*; threats to sever diplomatic relations with France over the latter's parliamentary declaration that there was such a genocide; replacing the Turkish Prime Minister's Renault with an inferior Russian limo; Sydney Turks demanding that the broadcaster SBS [Scandinavian Broadcasting Systems] pulp its 25th anniversary history for twice making passing reference to an event they claim "never happened"; and, more recently, frenetic Turkish efforts to stop a memorial to the dead Assyrians in the western Sydney district of Fairfield.

Explanations abound. One is that turkey is the victim of the single greatest conspiracy in world history, with states such as Belgium, Brazil, Canada, Chile, France, Germany, Holland, Italy, Northern Ireland, Poland, Russia, Scotland, Sweden, Switzerland, the Vatican and Wales conniving to falsely brand Turkey as a genocidaire. Another is that somehow 11 million Armenians around the globe have subverted the truth, history and dozens of nations to "frame" innocent Turkey. Yet another is that witnesses—such as British historians Arnold Toynbee and Viscount [James] Bryce, German missionary Dr Johannes Lepsius and German medico Armin Wegner, the American ambassador to Turkey Henry Morgenthau and his Swedish diplomatic colleagues—invented their sometimes daily conversations with the major perpetrators, Talaat Pasha and Enver Pasha, and lied to besmirch Turkish honour. Another is that the dozens of Australian POWs [prisoners of war], isolated and often grossly maltreated in remote villages rather than in camps, deliberately faked the photographs and invented the atrocity stories they brought back home. They assert that the special Turkish military courts-martial held in Istanbul in 1919 only sentenced several perpetrators to death in absentia and imprisoned some 30 others for war crimes only because of duress from the Allies. The best explanation is that the Turks did precisely what they were recorded and filmed as doing, for which their own tribunals convicted them.

> *Even if today's Turkey decided to become more rather than less secular ... more willing to address its past in relation to Christians generally, the juggernaut of the denialism industry is such that it simply cannot stop.*

We are approaching a serious junction: The path to Gallipoli grows in scale and traffic each year, but so does the avenue to official recognition that what occurred was genocide, one in so many ways the prologue to, and template for, the Holocaust less than 20 years later. Sooner rather than later the US Congress will find the numbers for the two-thirds majority needed for recognition. The British government won't be far behind. More Australian states will follow and, inevitably, an unwilling (and very unhappy) federal government will have to do so. Our dilemma will be profound.

Acknowledge the Truth

There is, of course, a way forward: an admission of truth about the events; a genuine opening of all the Ottoman archives to obviate the old Turkish chestnuts about "awaiting the verdict of historians" and "Armenian revolutionaries engaged in civil war"; an offer of regret, or apology, even one leavened by a limitation on reparations. That way Turkey can more readily enter the European Union and the comity of nations. But the hysterical and obsessive denialism of the Batak

Who Are the Armenians?

The Armenians are an ancient people who have existed since before the first century C.E. Armenia has gained and lost a tremendous amount of territory throughout its long and turbulent history. Boundaries of the past have extended from that of the present-day Republic of Armenia and through most of modern-day Turkey. . . .

Although Armenia was at times a kingdom, in modern times, Armenia has been an independent country for only a few years. It first gained independence in 1918, after the defeat of the Ottoman Empire in World War I, but this ended when Armenia was invaded by the Red Army and became a Soviet state in 1920. With the dissolution of the Soviet Union in 1991, Armenia was the first state to declare its independence, and remains an independent republic today. Armenia is a democracy and its borders only include a very small portion of the land that was historic Armenia.

Sara Cohan,
"A Brief History of the Armenian Genocide,"
Social Education, *vol. 69, no. 6, October 2005.*

massacres in Bulgaria in 1876, the 200,000 Armenians dead at the hands of Sultan Abdul Hamid II between 1894 and 1896, the 1.5 million dead at the hands of the Young Turks from 1915, will always get in the way of "normal" relationships.

Even if today's Turkey decided to become more rather than less secular, more West-oriented, less cosy with Syria, Iran and Hezbollah in a jihadist worldview, more willing to address its past in relation to Christians generally, the juggernaut of the denialism industry is such that it simply cannot stop.

The machine has developed its own mind, its own convulsive and reflexive responses. Turks see genocide as a blot on their escutcheon and honour; they see themselves as decent people, and decent people don't commit genocide. Wrong. "Decent people"—like Americans, Canadians, Belgians, Italians, Germans, Austrians, Spaniards and Australians—have all done just that.

The Srebrenica Massacre Fits the Definition of Genocide

M.S.

M.S. is a correspondent for the Economist. *In the following viewpoint, the author contends that despite some recent controversy over the suitability of the word "genocide" to describe the Srebrenica massacre in Bosnia, it seems like the most common-sense term for what happened. Recent critics have pointed out that because Serb forces killed only the Muslim men at Srebrenica—and spared the women and small children—that the massacre does not fit the international definition of genocide. There might be a danger, however, to applying too narrow a definition of the term to what seems a pretty clear genocidal act, maintains the author.*

As you read, consider the following questions:

1. How many Bosnian Muslim men were murdered by Serb forces, according to the author?
2. What does the author say William Schabas is arguing about the Srebrenica genocide?
3. Why does the author believe that the Nazi case influences contemporary attitudes on genocide?

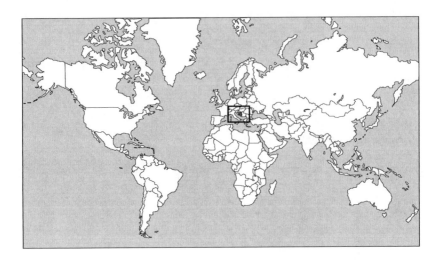

When I have one sentence to summarise what Ratko Mladic is on trial for, I start with "genocide". I follow with "war crimes and crimes against humanity", but I start with "genocide" because it's the best attention-grabber. And in the demotic man-on-the-street understanding of what constitutes genocide, ordering the massacre of 7,000 Bosnian Muslim men as part of a long campaign to drive the Bosnian Muslims out of Bosnian Serb-held territory doesn't seem to stretch the definition too much. So, as a reporter with 450 words to work with, that's what I use. It's perfectly correct: the 11 counts against Mr Mladic include genocide, and it's the prosecutors of the International Criminal Tribunal for the former Yugoslavia (ICTY) who made that call, not me.

But there is, as we report this week [June 2011], a serious case that use of the term "genocide" to apply to the massacres at Srebrenica, or to ethnic cleansing in Bosnia in general, is misplaced. The best-known fellow making this case is William Schabas, one of the world's foremost experts on international humanitarian law and author of *Genocide in International Law: The Crime of Crimes*. Mr Schabas thinks prosecutors had to stretch the definition of genocide to make it fit Srebrenica, as it's not clear that what Bosnian Serb leaders and commanders were doing was trying to eliminate the Bosnian Muslim people as such. He thinks that while the slaughter in Rwanda was a case of true genocide, the atrocities committed in the Yugoslavia war are best treated as crimes against humanity and war crimes, to avoid muddying the waters and setting bad precedents for future prosecutions. For his troubles, he has found himself denounced as a "genocide denier", which is clearly silly.

It's . . . plausible to find the overall campaign to eliminate the Muslim populations of the self-proclaimed Bosnian Serb republic to be genocide.

Defining Genocide

Still, I'm not sure I agree with the argument. Katherine G. Southwick made the case this way, in an article in the *Yale Human Rights and Development Law Journal* criticising the *Krstic* decision [referring to the decision in the ICTY case *Prosecutor v. Radislav Krstic*], in which the ICTY first found that Srebrenica was genocide:

> According to the International Law Commission, "the distinguishing characteristic" of the crime of genocide is the element of specific intent, which requires that certain acts be "committed with intent to destroy, in whole or in part, a national, ethnical, racial or religious group, as such." By excluding consideration of the perpetrators' motives for killing the military-aged men, such as seeking to eliminate a military threat as the defense alleged, the *Krstic* chamber's standard for establishing specific intent to destroy the Bosnian Muslims, in whole or in part, was incomplete. In addition, stretching the meaning of certain terms in the definition, such as a group "in part" and "destroy," also suggests a misapplication of the word "genocide." In effect, adopting an

interpretation of genocide that cannot and will not be universally applied, the chamber untenably broadened the meaning of the term.

Ms Southwick points out, following the defence's arguments, that Mr Mladic's forces at Srebrenica not only didn't kill the Muslim women and children at Srebrenica; they took the time and expense to separate them out and transport them to Muslim lines. Why would they have done that, if their intent was to annihilate the entire Muslim population? It seems much more plausible that they intended, as they said, to eliminate the men as potential combatants. Slaughtering captives is an abominable war crime nonetheless, but it's not necessarily genocide. To get around this, the court ruled that killing the men and deporting the women and children was clearly intended to eliminate the Muslim population *of Srebrenica*, which met the standard of eliminating Bosnian Muslims "in part". This does seem like a bit of a dodge.

A Commonsense Application

Still, though, I'm not sure I would toss out the commonsense application of "genocide" to Srebrenica. That massacre didn't occur in isolation. It was the most gruesome episode of mass slaughter in a conscious campaign of ethnic cleansing that began when Slobodan Milosevic started talking about "Greater Serbia" and proclaiming that "wherever there is a Serb, there is Serbia", implying that Muslims who happened to inhabit intrinsically Serbian areas would have to be gotten rid of. The Serbian ethnic-cleansing campaign in Bosnia, run consciously by Radovan Karadzic and Ratko Mladic, entailed rounding up Muslim civilians, killing or burning out the ones who refused to go, and shipping many off to concentration camps, with all the associated torture and mass rape one might expect. A finding of genocide due to an attempt to eliminate the Muslims of Srebrenica may be a bit dodgy, but it's a lot more

Ratko Mladic Arrested

"Ratko Mladic Arrested," cartoon by BART, www.CartoonStock.com. Copyright © BART. Reproduction rights obtainable from www.CartoonStock.com.

plausible to find the overall campaign to eliminate the Muslim populations of the self-proclaimed Bosnian Serb republic to be genocide. Perhaps Mr Mladic didn't intend to annihilate every Bosnian Muslim, including those in Sarajevo; but I don't think the Ottomans ever wanted to kill the Armenians in Armenia. And the Interahamwe didn't try to kill the Tutsi in Burundi.

I think one runs the risk here of a more common problem: letting an idea of evil formed in response to the Nazis hew so narrowly to the specific, extremely weird Nazi case that it becomes practically useless in the course of general history. The Nazis were extremely strange, and their determination to annihilate the Jewish race as such wherever it might be found on hallucinatory pseudo-scientific grounds was insane. You're not going to come across events that fit that specific profile very often. But the Nazis were also a particularly crazy case of a more frequent type of political monstrosity that one encounters very often, notably in central, southern and eastern Europe in the last century: mass slaughter intended to wipe out or drive out some population in the service of the political hegemony of a charismatic populist party with an ethnic, religious, racial or class-based identity. That's a problem that we're going to encounter over and over again, not just in Europe. The term "genocide" seems like a good description, and if courts need to do a little work to show how the crime fits the definition sometimes, I'm not too troubled by that.

Lithuania's Push for a Genocide Law Is Appalling

Jonathan Freedland

Jonathan Freedland is a journalist and weekly columnist for the Guardian *as well as a prolific author. In the following viewpoint, he explains his opposition to Lithuania's double genocide approach, which aims to place the crimes of the Soviet occupiers during the Cold War on par with the Holocaust carried out during World War II by the Nazi occupiers. Freedland argues that there is no symmetry between the two: The Holocaust was a systematic genocidal campaign to murder Jews; the other was the repression and silencing of political enemies. In addition, Freedland also finds that Lithuanians tend to ignore their own complicity in the Holocaust and want to create a myth of victimhood that they can use against their current nemesis, Russia.*

As you read, consider the following questions:

1. To what event does the Great Action refer, according to the author?

2. What percentage of Lithuania's Jews were killed by Nazis and Lithuanian volunteers?

3. According to Freedland, what is on display at the Museum of Genocide Victims in Vilnius?

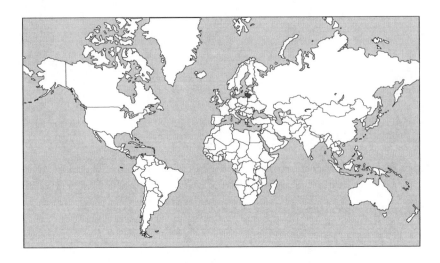

No one wants to live surrounded by death. It's understandable that people who now live on the spot that was once the Kovno ghetto, where close to 35,000 Jews were herded, starved and eventually led to their deaths, would not want to be constantly reminded of the fact. So I was not too surprised this week [in September 2010] to watch fathers pushing baby buggies and mothers carrying groceries on Linkuvos Street, a residential road in modern Kaunas, Lithuania, with just one small obelisk—barely visible amid the traffic at a junction—marking the site where the gates to the ghetto once stood. The wording, in Hebrew and Lithuanian, is brief: no death toll, no mention of the unspeakable suffering that happened within.

I understand, too, why there are no special road signs directing visitors to make the short drive to the Ninth Fort, the place where the Nazis and their Lithuanian collaborators dug deep, vast pits—into which they shot almost 10,000 Jews, including 4,273 children, on a single day in October 1941, the so-called Great Action. I can see why the people of Kaunas would prefer the Ninth Fort to be seen only by those people who come looking for it.

Memory and history never belong solely in the past; they are contested in the here and now, as freighted with politics as any other aspect of the present. So it is in Lithuania, which, along with neighbouring Latvia and Poland, had a walk-on part in British politics last year [2009], when [British Prime Minister] David Cameron came under fire for partnering his MEPs [members of the European Parliament] with assorted ultra-nationalist fringe parties from eastern Europe. This week, searching along with my father for the roots of our family—one branch of which once lived in the Lithuanian village of Baisogala—I had a chance to examine what had once been a faraway Westminster battle on the ground and up close.

A More Recent Memorial

I have now seen for myself, for example, that the Ninth Fort includes not only a massive, Soviet-era socialist-realist memorial to the dead buried in those pits, but a newer exhibition hall, covering the oppression of the Soviet years—even though the connection between subject and location is tenuous at best. Of course, I can see why Lithuanians want to remember the era of the Gulag [Soviet forced labor camps] and forced exile to Siberia. It was more recent than the Second World War; it lasted longer; and it affected families still living in Lithuania. Besides, for four postwar decades to speak of that pain was forbidden, leaving a yearning for commemoration and recognition.

Pushing myself hard, I could almost empathise with the "double genocide" approach, officially endorsed in Lithuania and other former Soviet lands, which holds that Nazism and Communism were twin evils of the 20th century and ought to be remembered alongside each other—an approach embodied by the Ninth Fort, with its double museums, one recording the horrors of [German dictator Adolf] Hitler, the other counting the crimes of [Soviet dictator Joseph] Stalin.

After all, this is not a competition—and if it is, it's not one any Jew would want to win. Jews don't want or need a monopoly on grief. Tears are not in finite supply: There are more than enough to go around.

The Problem with the Double Genocide Law

But, no matter how great an effort of empathy I make, I cannot go along with the "double genocide", especially not now that I've seen how it plays out in practice rather than in theory. For one thing, the equation of Nazi and Communist crimes rarely entails an honest account of the former. The plaque at the Ninth Fort, for instance, identifies the killers only as "Nazis and their assistants". It does not spell out that those assistants were Lithuanian volunteers, enthusiastically murdering their fellow Lithuanians. In my travels, visiting a whole clutch of sites, I did not encounter one that gave a direct, explicit account of this bald, harsh truth: that Lithuania's Jews were victims of one of the highest killing rates in Nazi Europe, more than 90%, chiefly because the local population smoothed the Germans' path. Indeed, they began killing Jews on June 22, 1941, before Hitler's men had even arrived.

> *The oppression of the Soviet years was terrible, but it was not genocide: to be arrested is not to be shot into a pit.*

Second, even if the theoretical intention is to remember a "double genocide", it rarely stays double for very long. Take the Museum of Genocide Victims, off Vilnius's central Gedimino Boulevard. You would think such a place would feature the genocide of which Vilnius was close to the centre, namely the slaughter of the Jews. But you'd be wrong. The Holocaust is not mentioned. The focus is entirely on the suffering inflicted by the KGB [Soviet security agency]. Outside, there are two prominent stone memorials for Moscow's victims. If you wish to remember Lithuania's 200,000 slain Jews, you have to wander far from the main drag, up a side street, to the tiny Green House—which is anyway closed for renovation and whose director, under pressure from state officials, is fighting for her job.

It's the same story with a 2008 change in the law that, in the name of equivalence, banned not just Nazi symbols but Soviet ones too. As if that were not bad enough—banning a veteran of the anti-Hitler resistance from parading his medals—in May, a Lithuanian court held that the swastika was not a Nazi symbol after all, but part of "Baltic culture" and therefore could be displayed in public.

A False Symmetry

Even if the authorities were rigorous in maintaining a balance, and telling both stories honestly, I would still reject this "double genocide". For the symmetry here is false. No one wants to top the persecution league table, but nor can one accept that those who were "arrested, interrogated and imprisoned"—to quote the Vilnius museum—suffered the same fate as those Jews who were murdered, despite the exhibit's attempt to equalise them under the bland umbrella term "losses". The oppression of the Soviet years was terrible, but it was not genocide: to be arrested is not to be shot into a pit. They are different and to say otherwise is to rob "genocide", a very specific term, of all meaning.

Finally, there is a sinister undertone to all this equivalence talk. Professor Egidijus Aleksandravicius of Vytautas Magnus University in Kaunas told me that many Lithuanians like to imagine that if their forebears killed Jews it was only as "revenge" for all that Communists (for which read Jews) had inflicted on them. On this logic—warped because Soviet rule hit Jews as hard as anyone else—the "double genocide" in effect says: You hurt us, we hurt you, now we're even.

A Poisonous Notion

Why has this poisonous idea taken such deep root? Dovid Katz, who taught Yiddish at Vilnius University until his contract was not renewed this year, suspects geopolitics: "It supplies a massive stick with which to beat today's Russia," he says. Lithuania wants its European Union partners to see Moscow as a genocidal regime that has not made restitution.

He detects another motive too: The nationalist desire for Lithuanians to see themselves as a pristine people, free of stains on their record. Admitting the truth of the wartime past threatens that; insistence on victim status preserves it.

This may inform the action the rest of the world should take. Professor Aleksandravicius calls for a "soft hand", for outsiders to understand how psychologically difficult it is for people to realise that victims can be perpetrators too, to accept that having suffered in the first Soviet rule of 1940–41, "Lithuanians turned on the weakest people of all, the Jews".

I respect that approach: Memory is a sensitive business. But governments will have to speak more forcefully. Lithuania is in the EU [European Union] and NATO [North Atlantic Treaty Organization]: Its partners in those bodies have a duty to tell Vilnius plainly that it needs to reckon with its past truthfully, no matter how painful that may be. Only then will the haunting spirits of the past let it rest.

Periodical and Internet Sources Bibliography

The following articles have been selected to supplement the diverse views presented in this chapter.

Erica Alini	"The Trouble with 'Double Genocide,'" *Maclean's*, January 12, 2011.
BBC News	"Analysis: Defining Genocide," August 27, 2010.
Robert Fisk	"Living Proof of the Armenian Genocide," *Independent* (UK), March 9, 2010.
Michael Ignatieff	"The Limits of Good v. Evil," *National Post*, September 30, 2011.
Emmanuel Jarry	"Sarkozy Challenges Turkey to Face Its History," Reuters, October 6, 2011. http://uk.reuters.com.
Tony Monda	"Ethnocide of the Ba Tonga Art," *Herald* (New Zealand), October 14, 2011.
Eric Reeves	"Are U.S. and U.N. Officials Ignoring New Evidence of Atrocities in Sudan?," *New Republic*, July 23, 2011.
Harut Sassounian	"96 Years Later, Turkey Still Pays a Price for Genocide Denial," *Asbarez*, October 18, 2011.
David Smith	"MDC Minister Compares Zimbabwe to Rwanda Before Genocide," *Guardian* (UK), June 8, 2011.
Sabrina Tavernise	"Nearly a Million Genocide Victims, Covered in a Cloak of Amnesia," *New York Times*, March 9, 2009.

GLOBALVIEWPOINTS

CHAPTER 2

Contemporary Accounts of Genocide

The Democratic Republic of the Congo Is Devastated by Chronic Genocide

Georgio Trombatore

Georgio Trombatore is a correspondent for Secondo Protocollo, a human rights organization. In the following viewpoint, he describes the terrible situation unfolding in the Democratic Republic of the Congo as a chronic genocide perpetrated by numerous armed groups operating in the provinces of North Kivu, South Kivu, and Orientale. Trombatore reports that civilians are being targeted by the Ugandan rebel group known as the Lord's Resistance Army (LRA) as well as other smaller armed groups. Also perpetrating mass killings and rape are the Congolese army, the Ugandan military, and even corrupt members of the United Nations, the author asserts.

As you read, consider the following questions:

1. How does the author say that Oxfam International was treating the cholera crisis in the Democratic Republic of the Congo?
2. Who do the authorities think committed the mass rapes in Fizi in June 2011?

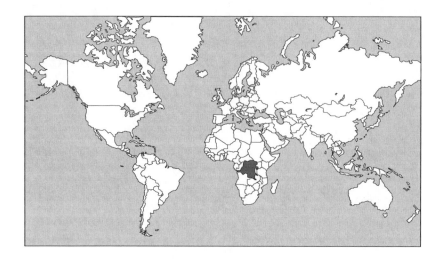

3. How many Congolese are estimated by the author to be dead?

Recently, [there has been] extensive use of the word "genocide", often even if there is a reason that justifies this real ugly word. But never a word was more appropriate than [in] the Democratic Republic of [the] Congo [DRC], where there is a chronic condition that genocide has been going on for decades, so that is no longer even news.

Mass rapes, torture unspeakable, killing on a large scale, small wars between powerful groups or between local rebels and the army for control of resources (gold, diamonds and coltan to name but three), or simple murder and violence without any good reason. This is the dramatic picture of the DRC which is added to a health situation that goes beyond the dramatic, which in recent weeks [in mid-2011] has seen an epidemic of cholera that has claimed . . . dozens of victims. Below is a brief report [that] anticipates the 10-day publication of a more detailed report on the actual situation in the Democratic Republic of [the] Congo and on the black market of coltan.

Disease and Violence in Massive Proportions

Cholera. Cholera is just the latest calamity that has hit this tormented land. To be affected were the provinces of Bandundu, Équateur and Kinshasa. As of June 30 [2011] was undoubtedly the hardest hit in Bandundu province where they recorded 1,048 cases of infection and 55 deaths. At the same time in the province of Équateur were recorded 324 cases and 23 deaths. To address the situation the NGO [nongovernmental organization] Oxfam [International] has sent an emergency mission that will be tasked to monitor the situation and provide 25 points of access to clean water. Oxfam is also looking for a solution that helps to purify and extract clean water from many wells in the area. As well as Oxfam are also moving to the World Health Organization (WHO), UNICEF [United Nations children's fund] and the NGO Médecins Sans Frontiéres (MSF) [also known as Doctors Without Borders].

Violence in South Kivu Province. According to several complaints on 11 and 12 June [2011] there were several cases of mass rape in the town of Fizi already hard hit by an attack on 18 May by the Rwandan rebel group FDLR (Democratic Forces for the Liberation of Rwanda) who had taken dozens of casualties and terror among the population. It is not yet clear who carried out mass rapes even though it seems fairly certain that it is always the FDLR. A mission of the United Nations and other humanitarian organizations arrived in Fizi June 25 just with the aim of establishing the facts and bringing a first aid (including psychological) to victims of mass rapes. Doctors Without Borders says that only the date of 22 June has provided assistance to more than 100 women victims of rape. Mass rape in eastern Congo is unanimously considered a true "non-conventional weapon." But in addition to the FDLR in South Kivu region of many other acts that cause violence and armed groups, consequently, large movements of people fleeing from their own violence. In recent weeks there have been large movements of people [from] Fizi [and] Kabimba directed to the province of Katanga. The displaced are thousands only in recent weeks. Other significant movements of people are reported in the territory of Shabunda. The NGO Malteser International has denounced the presence of over 1,800 displaced families in the areas of Kigulube and Nzibira. But [it is] not enough [that there are a] number of irregular armed groups, violence is reported also by regular Congolese army. It should be noted in particular the forced recruitment of children in the city of Nyamarhege, while a hundred students of a primary school [in the] area of Shabunda of Congolese have been forced by the military to carry military equipment, including explosives and ammunition, for five miles.

The genocide in the Democratic Republic of [the] Congo has become chronic, almost a normal thing for Western countries and global institutions.

North Kivu. The violence in recent months [that] had forced several NGOs to leave the territory of North Kivu at the moment seems diminished so much that in July the NGO Save the Children UK (SC-UK) will resume operations in the area of nutritional. . . . The World Health Organization [WHO] reports that dozens of cases of measles were reported in the Ubundu. The WHO in collaboration with several NGOs is preparing a vaccination campaign against this disease that affects thousands of people each year in North Kivu, claiming hundreds of lives. Cases of cholera have been reported in North Kivu. In this regard, the International Red Cross in collaboration with the CRI [Country of Return Information Project] of Congo is preparing three sources of drinking water in areas Sabasaba and Dongo. . . . There remains the problem of systematic use of children in the extraction and transport of precious minerals and their intensive smuggling by armed groups.

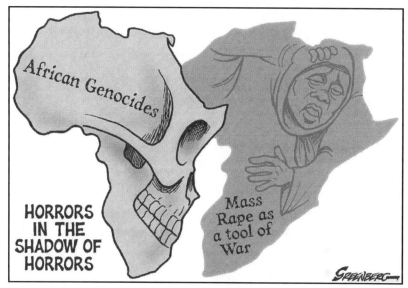

"Horrors in the Shadows of Horrors," cartoon by Bart, www.CartoonStock.com. Copyright © BART. Reproduction rights obtainable from www.CartoonStock.com.

The Orientale Region

Violence in Orientale Region.... The Ugandan rebel group Lord's Resistance Army (LRA) continues unabated in its attacks on civilians, starting from its bases that are located within the Garamba [National] Park. In this region, particularly in the area to the east, the lack of institution is felt. In addition to the LRA in the area there are also other smaller armed groups that control the coltan and diamond mines and forced the inhabitants to work in conditions of slavery. They are joined on and off, by corrupt military of the United Nations and the Ugandan military that engage in Congo under the pretext of chasing the leader of the LRA, Joseph Kony, the reason given by the military even south Sudanese. Eventually in this clash of military and militia are to be entered incredible violence against civilians. Mass rapes, the abduction of children to make child soldiers, sexual slaves or slaves for the mining of diamonds and coltan, unspeakable torture and indiscriminate killings. In recent weeks thousands of people have put in motion towards the region of Équateur, considered safer, causing a huge influx of refugees in particular in the town of Bumba. The government of the Democratic Republic of [the] Congo has committed months ago to regain control of the region and the mines, promising ... not [to] use children for the extraction of minerals and that it would guarantee the rights of workers, but at present this [has] not yet happened. Indeed, [there] were reported several cases of corruption among the ranks of government officials and even the few UN military forces in the region. The rebel groups, well-financed primarily from the sale of diamonds and coltan, completely control the region without anyone to do something to bring a modicum of legality.

Estimating the Loss

It is not possible to determine how many deaths [result from] this situation (because official data are lacking), but it is estimated that over the years, the micro-conflicts that have affected and conflicts affecting the regions of South Kivu, North Kivu and Orientale, ... cost over four million dead and millions displaced. A genocide is completely forgotten by all, genocide still going on, even if the mainstream press does not mention it. The genocide in the Democratic Republic of [the] Congo has become chronic, almost a normal thing for Western countries and global institutions. It [is] obvious that [it] is convenient [for no one] to change the state of things, especially at a time when the demand for coltan and other minerals essential to modern technologies has skyrocketed. Therefore, it becomes increasingly necessary to approve the protocol for the certification of origin of coltan, a system within a few months should not only regulate the trade of precious ore, but also its removal, which must be in compliance with fundamental human rights.

Western Sahara Genocide Is Being Ignored by the European Union

Airy Sindik Mejia Lara

Airy Sindik Mejia Lara is a correspondent for The Prisma. *In the following viewpoint, Lara points out that the people of Western Sahara have been waiting for thirty-five years for independence and have gotten only exploitation, brutality, and oppression in return. Moroccan forces have raped, tortured, persecuted, and slaughtered the Saharan people for years, Lara explains, while the countries of the European Union have ignored the injustice. After being ignored for so long, it would not be surprising if the people of Western Sahara were to take up arms to claim their independence from failed colonial powers, the author concludes.*

As you read, consider the following questions:

1. According to the author, of what natural resource does Western Sahara hold 85 percent?

2. How long does the author say that the United Nations Mission for the Referendum in Western Sahara remained in Western Sahara?

3. What did France do at the meeting of the UN Security Council on November 16, 2010, according to the author?

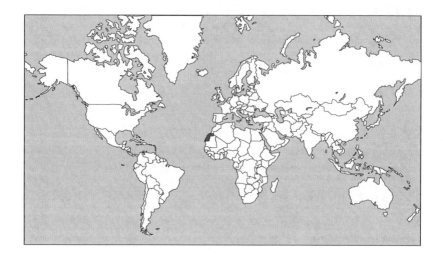

It is bordered to the south by Mauretania, to the north by Morocco and to the east by Algeria. Its territory is the Sahara Desert and its capital is El Ayoun, near the sea in the north.

In Western Sahara there are natural resources including 85% of the world's stock of phosphate, used in the production of agrochemicals, one of the most destructive of industries.

But this is not the only resource that is found in this forgotten territory; there are also oil, gas, the biggest fish stocks in the world, and the richest fosses of water in North Africa.

Europe has profited from these since the territory was proclaimed a colony by Spain in 1885, and more extensively since its occupation in 1934. Years have gone by for this land and no one has stopped lying about the Sahrawi people.

The Promise of Independence

During the time of [Francisco] Franco's dictatorship, on the 17th and 18th of July 1936, while he was planning his coup against the Spanish Republic, he promised independence for the Sahrawi people in exchange for their support.

Deceived and still dreaming of independence, they began the first rebellions against the Republican government in the

African colonies of Spanish Sahara, Ceuta, Melilla and Tetuán, from where boats later set sail in support of Franco.

Once in power, the dictator forgot his promises, which became the first betrayal. On the eve of Franco's death on November 14th 1975 the tripartite agreements were signed, selling Western Sahara to Morocco and Mauretania, the second betrayal.

During the transition from Francisco Franco's dictatorship to so-called democracy in Spain, King Juan Carlos promised independence, and once again betrayed the Sahrawi people, the third betrayal.

More Betrayals

On the 14th November 1976 Felipe González also promised independence, and when in power betrayed the Sahrawi people for the fourth time. In recent times [Spanish prime minister José Luis Rodríguez] Zapatero and [Spanish foreign affairs minister] Trinidad Jiménez declared themselves in favour of Saharan independence, and once in power created a strategy of censorship, and sold arms to support the Moroccan occupation of Saharan territory, the fifth betrayal.

In 1991 the United Nations promised to hold a referendum on self-determination and independence for the Sahrawi people within 8 months, in exchange for a cease-fire between the Polisario Front and Morocco.

Monarchy, dictatorship, the left, the right and the international agencies have betrayed Western Sahara and its people.

The United Nations Mission for the Referendum in Western Sahara (MINURSO), spent 18 years in the territory without making the slightest improvement in living conditions or human rights in the areas occupied by Morocco in Western Sahara, the sixth international betrayal.

Recent History of the Western Sahara

Morocco annexed the northern two-thirds of Western Sahara (formerly Spanish Sahara) in 1976 and claimed the rest of the territory in 1979, following Mauritania's withdrawal. A guerrilla war with the Polisario Front contesting Morocco's sovereignty ended in a 1991 UN [United Nations]-brokered cease-fire; a UN-organized referendum on the territory's final status has been repeatedly postponed. The UN since 2007 has sponsored intermittent talks between representatives of the government of Morocco and the Polisario Front to negotiate the status of Western Sahara. Morocco has put forward an autonomy proposal for the territory, which would allow for some local administration while maintaining Moroccan sovereignty. The Polisario, with Algeria's support, demands a popular referendum that includes the option of independence.

US Central Intelligence Agency, "Western Sahara,"
The World Factbook, *May 17, 2011.*

The Saharan people have been betrayed by all the different brands of Western ideologies.

Monarchy, dictatorship, the left, the right and the international agencies have betrayed Western Sahara and its people.

These are the so-called alternatives that the West has offered as a peaceful solution to the conflict, while in reality the agonising situation has been perpetuated.

A Terrible Genocide

The conditions which existed before the Saharan protest camp of Gdeim Izik, 15 km from the city of El Ayoun included: torture; disappearances; persecution; the rape of women and girls; the economic, political and cultural marginalization of the Sahrawi people; the razing to the ground of homes; plunder; a multitude of beatings; mass graves and 'black prisons', all at the hands of the occupying Moroccan police and armed forces.

Innumerable violations of human rights could be cited, but taken together the conditions during the last 35 years [before 2010] in the territories occupied by Morocco in Western Sahara amount to genocide, the attempted extermination of the Sahrawi people.

The Sahrawi protest camp at Gdeim Izik in Western Sahara, which lasted from its beginning on Oct. 9th until its violent eviction on November 8th was an ultimatum to the international community, to respond urgently, and they called for the Red Cross, UN peacekeepers, the international media and international human rights organizations. . . .

In Gdeim Izik the slogan of the Sahrawis was: "I don't want a house or a job, all I want is independence and for the Moroccans to leave".

The Role of the European Countries

At the meeting of the UN Security Council on Tuesday Nov. 16th 2010, the French response was once again to veto MINURSO so it does not have power concerning human rights.

Spain plays down the death and extermination of the Saharan people, prioritizing the economic and strategic interests of its friend Morocco.

London is paralysed by the student rebellion against the raising of university tuition fees. Milan finds itself hostage to mafia-dominated rubbish collectors, who blackmail the extreme-right government of [Italian prime minister Silvio] Berlusconi into brutally repressing protests.

Greece and Ireland face an economic crisis, and in Portugal a national strike has been announced. France has blue-collar workers on strike, while in Spain strikes by white-collar workers are ended by the army.

The European Union, championed by Germany, speculates with fishing rights and energy exploitation in this occupied territory of Western Sahara.

With the evidence contained in reports by Amnesty International and Human Rights Watch, the European Union hesitates to carry out an investigation of what happened during the eviction of Gdeim Izik, and later in El Ayoun, after nightfall during the military curfew, when there were tortures in public, and many murders in Saharan homes at the hands of the Moroccan police and occupiers.

The consequence of the European economic and political crisis is murder and genocide in Western Sahara. This is the price to be paid for a failed decolonization. We should not be surprised or shocked if all these betrayals leave the Saharan people only one alternative. 35 years of patience waiting for a peaceful decolonization process to happen is a lot of patience.

We are on the eve of war, and maybe the powerful in Europe are even hoping for it, to regenerate their economies.

The price of colonialism is war abroad. Convenience for Europe at the cost of concentration camps and military encampments in Western Sahara, to maintain the businesses that support the European Union. The economic crisis in Europe costs the most painful ruin in other countries. Here in Europe governments fall and politicians come and go. In Western Sahara the Sahrawi people's very existence as part of humanity is at stake. The West boasts of democracy while it exports battlefields. These are the consequences of a global system in crisis.

Sri Lanka Committed Genocide of Its Tamil Minority

Brian Senewiratne

Brian Senewiratne is a member of the Socialist Alliance in Brisbane, Australia. In the following viewpoint, he discusses the ongoing genocide of the Tamil people in Sri Lanka, perpetrated by the Sinhalese-dominated government. Senewiratne finds a religious element to the genocide, as the Buddhist Sinhalese, with the help of bigoted Buddhist monks, want to claim the country for Buddhism and drive out the Tamils, the majority of whom are Hindu. He points out that there are a number of ways to commit genocide, and the government seems intent on utilizing them all.

As you read, consider the following questions:

1. According to the author, when did Britian rule Sri Lanka?
2. What percentage of Sri Lanka does the author classify as Tamil?
3. How many Tamils does the author say have been driven out of Sri Lanka as of 2009?

There is a humanitarian crisis in Sri Lanka, where the Tamil minority in the island's north and east are facing annihilation at the hands of the Sinhalese-dominated government.

Brian Senewiratne, "Sri Lanka: Genocide of the Tamil Minority," GreenLeft.com, January 23, 2009. Copyright © 2009 by GreenLeft.com. All rights reserved. Reproduced by permission.

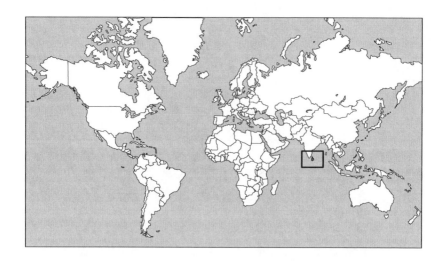

This [viewpoint] will deal with the current crisis, with the more fundamental problem of the legacy left by colonial British rule (1796–1948) dealt with in later articles. These colonial administrative structures will need to be reversed if there is ever to be peace or prosperity in Sri Lanka.

I am a Sinhalese, from the majority community, not from the brutalized Tamil minority. I quit Sri Lanka in 1976.

Who runs that country is of no concern to me, as long as it is run without serious violations of human rights. Sri Lanka was tossed out of the UN [United Nations] Human Rights Council in May last year [2008] due to its human rights record, and the drift of a democracy to a fascist politico-military dictatorship, none of which has been publicised internationally.

The Current Problem

The ethno-religious mix of Sri Lanka, with 20 million people, consists of ethnic Sinhalese (74%), Tamils (18%) in two groups (ethnic Tamils, 12.5%, and the plantation, or Indian, Tamils, 5.5%) and Moors (6.5%).

The ethnic Sinhalese and the ethnic Tamils have been in the country for at least 2500 years—the Tamils for probably much longer, given the proximity of Sri Lanka to south India from where the ethnic Tamils came.

The plantation Tamils are descendants of indentured labourers brought to the country by the British in the mid-1850s to work in the tea plantations in the central hills. The Moors are descendants of Arab traders from the 13th–15th century.

Sri Lanka is a multiethnic, multireligious, multilingual and multicultural country. Despite this, the Sinhala-Buddhist majority claims that Sri Lanka is a Sinhala-Buddhist country.

The ethnic conflict is between the Sinhalese-dominated government and the ethnic Tamils. The Sinhalese speak an Indo-Aryan language, Sinhalese, while the Tamils a Dravidian language, Tamil. The Moors are mainly Tamil-speaking but many are bilingual.

To add a religious dimension to an already existing ethno-linguistic one, the Sinhalese are Buddhist (70%) and the Tamils are Hindus. About 7% of each group has been converted to Christianity by Westerners. The Moors are mostly Muslims.

Sri Lanka is a multiethnic, multireligious, multilingual and multicultural country. Despite this, the Sinhala-Buddhist majority claims that Sri Lanka is a Sinhala-Buddhist country.

The Perpetrators of Persecution

The main proponents of this ethno-religious chauvinism are, firstly, the Buddhist monks who claim that Buddha on his death bed nominated Sri Lanka to be the custodian of his teaching, and secondly Sinhalese politicians across the entire political spectrum who have done so to gain the political support of the Sinhalese Buddhist majority to get into or remain in power.

The major Sinhalese political parties have competed with each other to discriminate against the Tamils in language, education and employment with the clear intention of getting the Sinhalese vote.

A third proponent is the Sinhalese-dominated Sri Lankan Armed Forces [SLA] (99% Sinhalese). The head of the SLA stated in an interview in September last year: "I strongly believe that this country belongs to the Sinhalese. . . ."

The real danger is that while the ethno-religious bigots among the Buddhist clergy and the Sinhalese political opportunists are not in a position to deliver an exclusively Sinhala-Buddhist nation, the SLA—equipped and supported by countries such as the US, China, India, Pakistan, Britain and Israel, for their own geopolitical/economic gains—do have that capacity.

If this means committing genocide against the Tamil people, the politico-military junta, which has the temerity to call itself the "Government of the Democratic Socialist Republic of Sri Lanka", is more than willing to do so.

The Problem of Ethnic Cleansing

There are four options to achieve an exclusively Sinhala-Buddhist Sri Lanka.

1. Drive them out of the country. Although 1.3 million have already [as of January 2009] been driven out, there are still 2 million left.

2. Make them "non-people", i.e., internal refugees. Currently, there are 500,000 Tamil civilians living in refugee camps in the Tamil north and east or have fled into the jungles in the north to escape SLA bombing. There are also 200,000 Tamil refugees in south India.

On November 19 [2008], Amnesty International USA, in a publication titled *Sri Lanka Government Must Act Now to Protect 300,000 Displaced*, stated: "In September 2008, the Sri Lankan government ordered the United Nations (UN) and

The Tamil People

Sri Lanka's first aborigines with continuous lineage are the Tamil people. It is not precisely known when they came to the island, but perhaps as many as 5000 years ago. Archaeologists date the first humans in Sri Lanka to some 34,000 years. Scientists call them Balangoda people, the name of the location where artifacts were found. These hunting-gathering cave dwellers have no current lineage.

Tamils were also known as Proto-Elamites or Ela. These people in Sri Lanka call themselves Eelam Tamils, meaning earthly people. Tamils speak a Dravidian language, which has no ties to other language families. It was, perhaps, associated with Scythians and Urals. The Dravidian language and Tamils originated, perhaps, from Sumer and Ur: the cradle of the first civilization, now Iran. The Sumer and Tamils formed the first language of protograms on clay tablets. Tamil inscriptions and literature are at least 2500 years old. Today, 100 to 200 million people speak Tamil.

The Christian Bible refers to Elam as maritime nations in various lands, each with a separate language. In the myth of Noah's Ark, Elam was thought to be a descendant of one of Noah's three sons on the ark. Tamils were the first to use the wheel for transportation. They traveled to India and the island of Sri Lanka, which had been connected to India. The first known manuscripts in India were written in Tamil. Other Tamil inscriptions have been found in Egypt and Thailand.

Ron Ridenour,
"Tamil Eelam: Historical Right to Nationhood, Part 2,"
Dissident Voice, *November 17, 2009.*

nongovernment aid workers to leave the region (the Tamil North). The government then assumed total responsibility for ensuring the needs of the civilian population affected by the hostilities are met."

On December 23, the US-based Human Rights Watch (HRW) came out with a detailed 49-page report entitled *Besieged, Displaced, and Detained.* The plight of civilians in Sri Lanka's Vanni region of the Sri Lankan government's responsibility for the plight of 230,000 to 300,000 displaced people in the Vanni (northern) conflict zone.

It documents that thousands of Tamils fleeing the fighting in the north are trapped by the government and are being denied basic provisions.

Brad Adams, HRW Asia director, one of the people who wrote this report, said: "To add insult to injury, people who manage to flee the fighting end up being held indefinitely in army-run prison camps."

He went on to make the situation abundantly clear: "The government's 'welfare centers' for civilians fleeing the Vanni are just badly disguised prisons."

3. Make them "disappear". Today, Sri Lanka leads the world in "involuntary disappearances".

On November 24, HRW published a report entitled *Sri Lanka: Human Rights Situation Deteriorating in the East* in which Adams stated: "The Sri Lankan government says that the 'liberated' East is an example of democracy in action and a model for areas recaptured from the LTTE [Liberation Tigers of Tamil Eelam]. But killings and abductions are rife, and there is total impunity for horrific acts."

4. Kill them—i.e., commit genocide. "Genocide" is defined by the UN Convention on the Prevention and Punishment of the Crime of Genocide as "an act committed with intent to destroy, in whole or in part, a national, ethnic, racial or religious group".

Committing Genocide

Genocide has nothing to do with numbers killed; it is the intention and the act(s) to achieve this intention that defines it.

Bombing, shelling and shooting are not the only ways to kill. One could starve them, withhold essential medicines, prevent survival activity (e.g., fishing and agriculture), destroy businesses, markets, homes, hospitals and schools. Once the intention is there, the ways to achieve genocide are endless.

There are also different types of genocide. I have called these, "educational genocide", "cultural genocide", "economic genocide" and "religious genocide"—defined as the intention, backed by the act, of destroying in whole or in part the education, culture or economy and religion of an ethnic group.

The Sri Lankan government is guilty of all of these.

Sudan's South Kordofan Province Is Devastated by a Renewed Genocide

Tristan McConnell

Tristan McConnell is GlobalPost's senior correspondent for Africa. In the following viewpoint, he passes along reports by aid workers in the South Kordofan province of the Sudan that government troops are slaughtering scores of ethnic Nubians in retaliation for siding with the South during the recent civil war. McConnell states that many people are concerned that the violence is bordering on a full-scale ethnic cleansing campaign and genocide of the Nubian people. The Sudanese government is justifying the widespread executions as the military response to a Nubian insurrection, McConnell maintains, but many believe it is a coldhearted, clear-eyed massacre of political enemies.

As you read, consider the following questions:

1. According to the author, how did the recent campaign of violence begin?
2. How many people fled the fighting in June 2011 in South Kordofan, according to the United Nations?
3. According to a leaked UN report, northern fighters were dressing up in the uniform of what aid group to round up and kill displaced Nubians?

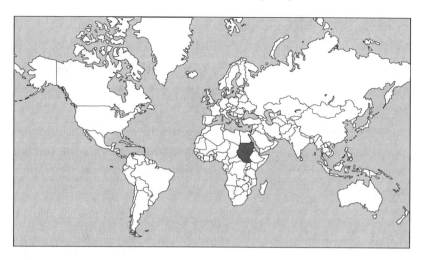

Systematic, brutal killings of hundreds of ethnic Nubians are being carried out by Sudanese forces loyal to President Omar al-Bashir's Khartoum [the capital of Sudan] regime, according to reports from the troubled South Kordofan province.

The reports of widespread murders akin to ethnic cleansing and even genocide were confirmed by an international aid worker who recently left South Kordofan and who told GlobalPost of credible accounts of scores of Nubian men, who supported the South during the civil war, being killed by northern Sudanese troops.

"They were executed, sometimes with a bullet in the head but often their throats were cut. You are forced onto the ground, a knee put in your back, your head lifted up and your throat slit, just like a goat," said the aid worker.

The aid worker, who has more than 20 years' experience in Sudan, did not want to be identified for security reasons—fearing that his account might endanger the lives of his friends and colleagues still in South Kordofan—but his description sheds a light on a conflict that bears the hallmarks of Bashir's genocidal war in Darfur, for which he has been indicted by the International Criminal Court (ICC).

A Plea for Help

Earlier this month [June 2011] the Anglican bishop of Kadugli, bishop of South Kordofan's main city and the epicenter of the fighting, issued a stark warning of the ethnic violence and a plea for help.

"Once again we are facing the nightmare of genocide of our people in a final attempt to erase our culture and society from the face of the earth," warned the Bishop Andudu Adam Elnail.

"It is not a war between armies that is being fought in our land, but the utter destruction of our way of life and our history, as demonstrated by the genocide of our neighbors and relatives in Darfur," he said.

"This is a war of domination and eradication, at its core it is a war of terror by the government of Sudan against their people," he said.

The Origins of the Recent Violence

The violence in South Kordofan started on June 5 [2011] with an artillery barrage targeting the Kadugli home and office of the state's most senior Sudan People's Liberation Movement (SPLM) official.

The assault came soon after the departure of Ahmed Haroun, the state's recently and controversially elected governor. Haroun, like Bashir, is wanted by the ICC for alleged war crimes committed in Darfur.

Northern soldiers backed by Antonov bombers and MiG fighter jets taking off from El Obeid airfield occupied parts of Kadugli city. Then, according to the aid worker, security forces went house to house dragging out opposition supporters, community leaders, intellectuals or anyone who was black.

The conflict is focused on the Nuba Mountains in the center of Sudan. Once a highland refuge from Arab slavers, the mountains more recently were the redoubt of the Nuba SPLM during the 22-year civil war that ended with a 2005 peace deal that will see the South secede early next month [July 2011].

With South Kordofan closed to outsiders no one knows how many have been killed, but reports of atrocities are trickling out.

The people of South Kordofan are northerners, except for the Nuba, who sided with the South during the civil war and who continue to protest their marginalization by Bashir's Islamist regime in Khartoum.

Bashir says his forces are putting down a rebellion in South Kordofan. The Nuba say they are fighting for their survival.

The Violent Conflict

The United Nations [U.N.] estimates that at least 73,000 have fled the fighting this month between Nuba fighters and the Sudanese army. With South Kordofan closed to outsiders no one knows how many have been killed, but reports of atrocities are trickling out.

Although impossible to confirm independently, reports from local residents say phosphorous bombs may have been used and there is talk of trucks loaded with young men being driven into the forest and returning hours later, empty.

A leaked U.N. report alleges that northern fighters masqueraded as Red Crescent workers to round up displaced people who were then marched away and other reports claim that civilians were executed outside the perimeter of the main U.N. base in Kadugli while peacekeepers cowered inside.

The aid worker told GlobalPost he thought "hundreds, possibly thousands" have already died.

"It's clear that anyone living in this area is fair game. Whether you're carrying a hoe or an AK-47 you are the enemy because they know everyone in those areas voted for the Nuba SPLM," he said.

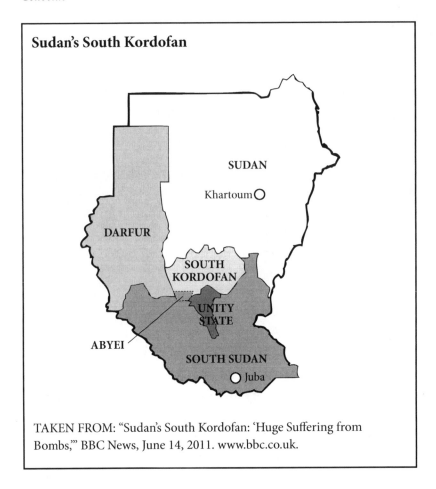

Sudan's South Kordofan

TAKEN FROM: "Sudan's South Kordofan: 'Huge Suffering from Bombs,'" BBC News, June 14, 2011. www.bbc.co.uk.

New Fears

He fears the current violence might outdo what he witnessed during the civil war.

"This is just the beginning. There is a huge concentration of troops, armored vehicles and tanks in Kadugli so it's clear that intensive land attacks are planned, a full onslaught. This is going to be much worse than the last war," he said.

He added that ethnically targeted killings had happened in the past, "but this is on a whole higher level of brutality, more of a planned operation."

The aid worker hesitated at labelling the killing genocide, but said that what is going on is bad enough, whatever it is called.

"This is mass murder based on ethnicity and political affiliation undertaken in broad daylight in barbaric ways and it's still going on," he said. "I spoke to a Nubian friend yesterday, he asked me, 'How many of us have to die before the international [community] will care?'"

Late on Tuesday [June 28, 2011], after more than three weeks of bloodshed, a deal was struck in Addis Ababa that called for northern-based soldiers of the Sudan People's Liberation Army (SPLA) to be integrated into Khartoum's army, offering a chance of peace in South Kordofan and Blue Nile state where thousands of SPLA fighters live.

However, the announced deal did not include a cease-fire so, for now, the war goes on and the killing continues.

Israel Is Committing an Ongoing Genocide of the Palestinian People

Maysaa Jarour

Maysaa Jarour is a correspondent for the Palestine Telegraph. *In the following viewpoint, she assesses the conflict between Israel and Palestine to determine whether there was, and still is, a genocide of the Palestinian people. Jarour outlines the defining characteristics of genocide and compares them to the circumstances of the founding of Israel and the 2008–2009 siege of Gaza, concluding that both situations fit the criteria of a genocidal campaign perpetrated by the Israelis. She argues that it is crucial to recognize, condemn, and fight genocide no matter the victim.*

As you read, consider the following questions:

1. According to the author, how many Jewish people were killed across Europe during the Holocaust?
2. Who does the author say coined the term "genocide"?
3. According to international agencies, what percentage of the deadly siege in Gaza were civilians?

I commemorated Holocaust Memorial Day with survivor Dr Hajo Meyer and some other Jewish friends after a talk at Goldsmiths University [of London] last week [February 2010].

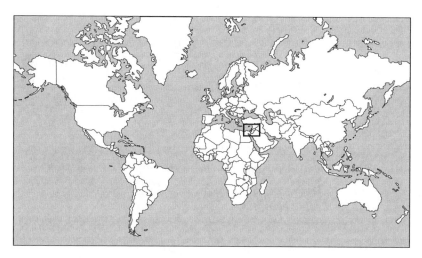

It is now clear to me that Palestinians have many common experiences with the survivors of the Holocaust.

Meyer's imprisonment in the ghetto and ordeal at checkpoints is a stereotypical image in occupied Palestine. I was amazed to hear him admit that the Palestinians' suffering is close to those who endured the Holocaust. I was also amazed because I heard it not from a Palestinian, but from a Jewish man who has suffered a lot.

For a long time, it has been widely argued that genocide has not been committed in Palestine. While some "left-leaning" media outlets say there was genocide, one that is still in progress, the Israeli narrative rejects the use of this term for the Palestinian experience. Without doubt, the Germans perpetrated genocide against the Jews in WWII. Around 6 million Jews were killed across Europe in an act that can never be tolerated by humanity. It is also a well-known fact, but rarely mentioned, that a total of over 50 million people, were either murdered or died from disease and starvation.

There have, however, been genocides against many other people, such as the American Indians, the Armenians and the South Africans, which must also be remembered. Unlike the Holocaust, most of these genocides are not as focused on.

Surely the fact that genocide has occurred must be condemned no matter who were the victims. Indeed, this seems to be the feeling of many Holocaust survivors themselves. They believe it is crucial to recognize, condemn and fight genocides wherever they are happening, no matter whether it involves a few thousand or millions.

According to the history of the founding of Israel, thousands of violent actions have been committed against one group of people: Palestinians.

A Palestinian Genocide?

The core question here is: Are the Palestinians suffering a genocide perpetrated by the government of Israel? (as many people believe). Has Israel attempted to ethnically cleanse Palestinians from their land? Is the term genocide legally applicable? Readers must make their own judgment.

In 1944, Polish-Jewish lawyer Raphael Lemkin coined the word "genocide" by combining "geno," from the Greek word for race or tribe, with "cide" from the Latin word for killing. He proposed that genocide consists of "a coordinated plan of different actions aiming at the destruction of essential foundations of the life of national groups, with the aim of annihilating the groups themselves."

Has this been happening in Palestine? According to the history of the founding of Israel, thousands of violent actions have been committed against one group of people: Palestinians. More than 535 villages were destroyed, thousands of residents were massacred and around 800,000 people were driven from their homes by force or fear of force. This process is described by Israeli historian Ilan Pappé and others as "the ethnic cleansing of Palestine." Since genocide is essentially the annihilation of a group, surely this is genocide.

On Dec. 9, 1948, the United Nations [UN] approved the Convention on the Prevention and Punishment of the Crime of Genocide. This convention established "genocide" as an international crime, which signatory nations "undertake to prevent and punish." It defines genocide this way: Genocide means any of the following acts committed with intent to destroy, in whole or in part, a national, ethnical, racial or religious group.

Killing Members of the Group

In 1948, thousands of Palestinians were exterminated by terrorist Jewish groups like the Stern, Haganah and Irgun. Other villagers were told to leave or they would be killed. The Deir Yassin massacre took place on April 9, 1948. More than 100 villagers, including women and children, were annihilated. Some were shot with live ammunition, while others burned to death as rockets rained down on the village. Prisoners were killed after being paraded through the streets in occupied Jerusalem; and it didn't stop in 1948. In 1956, a massacre of 500 villagers took place in Khan Younis in the middle of the Gaza Strip; others killed were Egyptians, who were policing the area at that time.

Causing Serious Bodily or Mental Harm to Members of the Group

The deadly siege in Gaza could easily be considered genocide according to this description. Bodily harm has been caused, not only during the siege or the last invasion (December 2008/January 2009), but since the beginning of the Israeli occupation of Palestine.

The overwhelming majority of the victims have been civilians, whereas only a small minority were resistance fighters. Some international agencies claim that 93 percent of those victimized were civilian, while only 7 percent were resistance fighters.

Organized and systematic attacks against civilians in Gaza are also part of the genocide. Several months before Operation Cast Lead, an Israeli minister even used the term "holocaust" to describe what was planned for the citizens of Gaza. On Feb. 28, 2008, the *Guardian*, BBC and other British media outlets reported the story under the headline: "Israeli minister warns of Palestinian 'holocaust.'" The *Guardian* reported that "an Israeli minister today warned of an increasingly bitter conflict in the Gaza Strip, saying the Palestinians could bring on themselves what he called a 'holocaust.'"

"The more Qassam [rocket] fire intensifies and the rockets reach a longer range, they will bring upon themselves a bigger shoah because we will use all our might to defend ourselves," Matan Vilnai, Israel's deputy defense minister, told Army Radio.

"Shoah" is the Hebrew word normally reserved to refer to the Jewish Holocaust. It is rarely used in Israel outside discussions of the Nazi extermination of Jews during the Second World War, and many Israelis are loath to countenance its use to describe other events.

Mental harm must also be considered. As pointed out in many UN agency reports, all Gazan children suffer mental and emotional problems. Stress and trauma make the children sick-minded due to constant fear. They have no opportunities for fun and joy, since the Israeli blockade even includes a ban on toys. It is not an exaggeration to say that a considerable number of the Gazan population is exhausted and mentally drained. They live with the constant realities of deprivation, war, restriction of freedom and death.

Inflicting Conditions of Life Calculated to Bring About the Group's Physical Destruction in Whole or in Part

This has been happening for years, ever since the establishment of the state of Israel. Focusing on the Gaza Strip today, the siege has impacted every aspect of life. Factories have stopped operating and food just trickles in. In addition, people have no freedom of movement beyond their "concentration camp," with just two gates that open irregularly.

The Israeli blockade on exports and on all but humanitarian imports has forced 98 percent of Gaza's industry to close. Around 1.5 million Palestinians live in just 360 square km, (139 square miles). More than three-quarters of the residents are refugees whose families were driven from their land, in what is now Israel, during the 1948 Arab-Israeli war.

The remaining two characteristics of what constitutes genocide include: imposing measures intended to prevent births within the group and transferring children of the group to another group. These remaining two characteristics were most evident in the 1948 Arab-Israeli war and the 1967 war.

Uganda Is Sanctioning a Gay Genocide

Sigrid Rausing

Sigrid Rausing is the publisher of Granta. *In the following viewpoint, she surveys the recent draconian bill proposed by a Ugandan lawmaker that looks to criminalize homosexuality and sanction a gay genocide. Rausing contends that the law reveals a profound misunderstanding of homosexuality because it is based on the premise that homosexuality is a choice, not a core personality trait. She notes Uganda's violent sexual history and culture and denounces even considering the death penalty for confirmed homosexuals that she calls a genocide of gay men and women.*

As you read, consider the following questions:

1. According to the author, consensual homosexual acts between adults are still illegal in how many countries?
2. According to the proposed law, what will happen to serial offenders who have a homosexual history in Uganda?
3. How long does the author say informers have to report homosexuals to authorities before they are charged with criminal behavior?

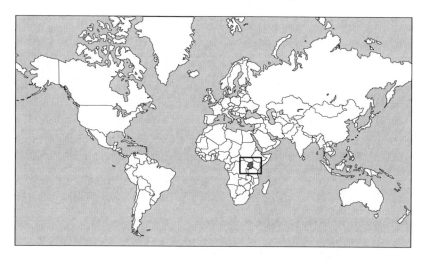

I recently reorganised the books in my study, and collected my remnants of feminist theory on a separate shelf; a fragment of another world. There were copies of *Feminist Review*, work by Betty Friedan, Simone de Beauvoir, Andrea Dworkin and Mary Daly. There was also [poet and writer] Adrienne Rich's pamphlet, "Compulsory Heterosexuality and Lesbian Existence", a dense and learned tract about the repression of lesbians.

Consciousness-raising made little distinction between street and boardroom thuggery and the effects of laws in repressive states. We didn't doubt Adrienne Rich when she said that lesbianism had been "crushed, invalidated, forced into hiding and disguise". We forgot the lesson of the Holocaust, which is that if the law and the power of the state supports discrimination and violence, you end up with genocide. Many minorities around the world still face discrimination, but only lesbians and gay men still face significant international legal discrimination.

Consensual homosexual acts between adults are still illegal in as many as 70 countries. Most countries have moved to a liberalisation of those unjust and repressive laws. In Uganda, however, the Hon David Bahati has sponsored an anti-homosexuality bill far more draconian than the already exist-ing code. It begins with principles and threats: the value of traditional family values, the threat of homosexual infection. The logic of the bill is this: "This legislation further recognizes the fact that same-sex attraction is not an innate and immu-table characteristic." But only if sexual orientation is voluntary can a person be held accountable for his or her choice. Sci-ence has concluded that sexual orientation is a core personal-ity trait, not a choice. You no more choose to be gay or bi-sexual than you choose to be left-handed or ambidextrous; it's a morally neutral position.

Category Mistake

Sexual expression and behaviour, however, is cultural and psy-chological, just like the expression of many other core person-ality traits. Innate traits express themselves in a multitude of ways, depending on the psychological, cultural and political environment. Cultures, like people, can be alcoholic (Soviet Russia), homosexual (ancient Greece), conformist or liberal, creative or stifling. Knowingly or unknowingly, homophobic governments make the category mistake of confusing core personality with cultural expression, criminalising, in the pro-cess, a fairly stable and substantial minority of any given population.

Perhaps, most importantly, failure to inform the authori-ties, within 24 hours, of suspected homosexuals is crimi-nalised.

In this case, Bahati wants to get rid of those pesky "sexual rights activists seeking to impose their values of sexual pro-miscuity", as well as gay pornographers and paedophiles. There is no distinction in his mind between people who fall in love with people of their own gender, and sexual sleaze and crime: It's all a filthy mess of HIV, pornography, Western values,

Homosexuality in Africa

Many Africans view homosexuality as an immoral Western import, and the continent is full of harsh homophobic laws. In northern Nigeria, gay men can face death by stoning. . . . A handful of Muslim countries, like Iran and Yemen, also have the death penalty for homosexuals. But many Ugandans said . . . that was going too far.

Jeffrey Gettleman,
"Americans' Role Seen in Uganda Anti-Gay Push,"
New York Times, *January 3, 2010.*

decadence, feminism and predation. The draft bill separates "the offence of homosexuality" from "aggravated homosexuality". The former is consensual but the bill addresses only the "offender", as though in gay relationships there is only ever a perpetrator and a victim:

1. a person commits the offence of homosexuality if

(a) he penetrates the anus or mouth of another person of the same sex with his penis or any other sexual contraption;

(b) he or she uses any object of sexual contraption to penetrate or stimulate sexual organ of a person of the same sex;

(c) he or she touches another person with the intention of committing . . . homosexuality.

2. a person who commits an offence under this section
shall be liable on conviction to imprisonment for life.

The second, more serious offence of "aggravated homosexuality" turns on the notion of the "serial offender", defined in the introduction to the law as "a person who has previous convictions of the offence of homosexuality or related offences". Anyone who is a confirmed gay man or lesbian and already has a sexual history faces the death penalty, alongside homosexual rapists and child abusers.

This is how the law will work: Victims are not to be penalised; they are to be assisted, and their identities protected. Judges may order that the offender has to pay them compensation. In addition, "aiding", "abetting" or "promoting" homosexuality becomes illegal. Perhaps, most importantly, failure to inform the authorities, within 24 hours, of suspected homosexuals is criminalised. The Ugandan people must turn informants—or risk jail. Lovers must choose between "victim" or "offender"; the former protected and paid, the latter imprisoned or killed.

A Culture of Violence

Criminalisation of homosexuals in Britain led to blackmail, prison sentences, hormonal "treatments", suicides, sexual repression and ruined lives. The Ugandan bill, however, like the Nazi laws before it, makes homosexuality punishable, ultimately, by death.

A decade ago [around 1999], I visited the vast refugee camps in the north of Uganda. The Lord's Resistance Army had been conducting murderous raids from their camps in Southern Sudan, abducting children. The abducted boys, brutalised and drugged, became soldiers; the girls were kept as slaves. I remember the fixed smiles of the girls who had managed to escape from captivity. I remember their drawings of killings and death. Sexual violence is everywhere in Uganda. This bill, too, is part of that culture. And what is the death penalty for homosexuality if not sexual murder? The state that sets out to purge the nation of homosexuality becomes, in the end, itself a sexual predator.

Periodical and Internet Sources Bibliography

The following articles have been selected to supplement the diverse views presented in this chapter.

Senia Bachir Abderahman	"A Young Girl's Life in a Refugee Camp," *Pambazuka News* (Africa), October 6, 2011.
BBC News	"UN Report Says DR Congo Killings 'May Be Genocide,'" October 1, 2010.
Michael Gerson	"The Worthy Mission to Get Joseph Kony," *Washington Post*, October 17, 2011.
Jeffrey Gettleman	"Congo Study Sets Estimate for Rapes Much Higher," *New York Times*, May 11, 2011.
Geoff Hill	"Rights Activists Warn of Genocide in Sudan," *Washington Times*, July 12, 2011.
Daniel Howden	"Southern Sudan Accuses North of Planning Genocide," *Independent* (UK), March 14, 2011.
Nikolaj Nielsen	"34 Years and Waiting," *Pambazuka News* (Africa), October 6, 2011.
Kristin Palitza	"No End to Mass Rapes: 'It's a Miserable Life,'" Inter Press Service, October 17, 2011. http://ipsnews.net.
Eric Reeves	"Genocide in Sudan: Is It Happening Again?," *New Republic*, June 20, 2011.
Jason Straziuso	"LRA: Rebels Worth Sending U.S. Troops to Africa?," CBS News, October 15, 2011.

Preventing and Prosecuting Genocide

Rwanda: Mixed Legacy for Community-Based Genocide Courts

Human Rights Watch

Human Rights Watch (HRW) is an international human rights organization. In the following viewpoint, the organization presents the findings of a 2011 report on the achievements of community-based courts, known as Gacaca *courts, to prosecute crimes related to the 1994 genocide in Rwanda. In HRW's assessment, the* Gacaca *courts have had a mixed legacy: They have rapidly processed tens of thousands of genocide cases, helped reduce the prison population, and illuminated many of the crimes that occurred in 1994; but also, the system has violations of due process and possible miscarriages of justice. HRW recommends a panel of professional judges to review some of the more controversial cases.*

As you read, consider the following questions:

1. According to Human Rights Watch, how many *Gacaca* courts have been set up since 2005?

2. How many cases related to the 1994 genocide have the *Gacaca* courts heard since 2005?

3. When does HRW say that the government amended the *Gacaca* law to exclude crimes by the ruling political party, the RPF (Rwandan Patriotic Front)?

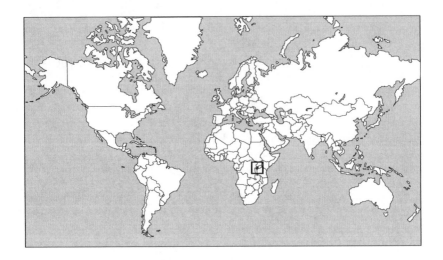

Rwanda's community-based *Gacaca* courts have helped communities confront the country's 1994 genocide but have failed to provide credible decisions and justice in a number of cases, Human Rights Watch said in a report released today. As the *Gacaca* courts wind down their work, Rwanda should set up specialized units in the national court system to review alleged miscarriages of justice, Human Rights Watch said.

The 144-page report, "Justice Compromised: The Legacy of Rwanda's Community-Based *Gacaca* Courts," assesses the courts' achievements and outlines a number of serious shortcomings in their work, including corruption and procedural irregularities. The report also examines the government's decision to transfer genocide-related rape cases to the *Gacaca* courts and to exclude from their jurisdiction crimes committed by soldiers of the Rwandan Patriotic Front (RPF), the country's ruling party since the genocide ended in July 1994.

"Rwanda's ambitious experiment in transitional justice will leave a mixed legacy," said Daniel Bekele, Africa director at Human Rights Watch. "The courts have helped Rwandans better understand what happened in 1994, but in many cases flawed trials have led to miscarriages of justice."

The report is based on Human Rights Watch observing over 2,000 days of *Gacaca* trials, reviewing more than 350 cases, and interviews with hundreds of participants from all sides of the *Gacaca* process, including accused persons, genocide survivors, witnesses, other community members, judges, and local and national government officials.

Since 2005, more than 12,000 community-based courts have tried 1.2 million cases relating to the 1994 genocide. The violence killed more than half a million people, mostly from the country's minority Tutsi population. The community courts are known as *Gacaca*—"grass" in the country's Kinyarwanda language, referring to the place where communities traditionally gathered to resolve disputes. The courts were scheduled to finish trials by mid-2010, but their closure was postponed in October 2010. In May 2011, the minister of justice reportedly announced that *Gacaca* courts would officially close by December 2011.

Gacaca courts were established in 2001 to address the overload of cases in the conventional justice system and a prison crisis. By 1998, 130,000 genocide suspects were crammed into prison space designed to accommodate 12,000, resulting in inhumane conditions and thousands of deaths. Between December 1996 and early 1998, conventional courts had tried only 1,292 genocide suspects, leading to broad agreement that a new approach was needed to speed up trials.

Rwandans have paid a high price . . . for the compromises made when setting up the new Gacaca *system.*

Rwanda's 2001 *Gacaca* law sought to resolve the bottleneck. The new *Gacaca* courts, with government oversight but limited due process guarantees, combined modern criminal law with more traditional informal community procedures.

The Rwandan government faced enormous challenges in creating a system that could rapidly process tens of thousands of cases in a way that would be broadly accepted by the population, Human Rights Watch said. The system's achievements include swift trials with popular participation, a reduction in the prison population, a better understanding of what happened in 1994, locating and identifying bodies of victims and a possible easing of ethnic tensions between the majority Hutu and minority Tutsi ethnic groups.

Rwandans have paid a high price, though, for the compromises made when setting up the new *Gacaca* system. Human Rights Watch found a wide range of fair trial violations. These included restrictions on the accused's ability to mount an effective defense; possible miscarriages of justice due to using largely untrained judges; trumped-up charges, some based on the Rwandan government's wish to silence critics; misuse of *Gacaca* to settle personal scores; judges' or officials' intimidation of defense witnesses; and corruption by judges and parties to cases.

"The creation of *Gacaca* was a good thing because it allowed the population to play a large role in the *Gacaca* process, but I deplore you [the judges] for taking sides," one witness testified at a trial attended by Human Rights Watch.

The Rwandan government contended that traditional fair trial rights were unnecessary because community members—familiar with what happened in their area in 1994—would expose false testimony or judicial bias. But Human Rights Watch found in many cases that potential witnesses failed to speak out in defense of genocide suspects because they feared prosecution for perjury, complicity in genocide, or "genocide ideology," a vaguely defined crime prohibiting ideas, statements, or conduct that might lead to ethnic tensions or violence. Others feared social ostracism for helping suspects defend themselves.

One genocide survivor interviewed by Human Rights Watch broke down in tears, saying he was ashamed he had

Independence and Impartiality of the *Gacaca* Process

Gacaca judges try cases relating to events that happened in their own area. Having lived through the genocide, many have their own strong views about what happened and know some or all the parties in any given case, whether they are relatives, friends, neighbors or business partners. Rwandan and international observers believe these factors have given rise to potential conflicts of interest or inherent partiality, and that with even the best will in the world, most *Gacaca* judges inevitably struggle to evaluate evidence impartially.

Gacaca has also seen widespread corruption and a pattern of political interference with the judiciary. Both phenomena occur in the conventional justice system too but appear to have been more pronounced in *Gacaca*. Judges were not the only ones who profited: Accused persons and genocide survivors also sought personal gain by engaging in corruption. At times local officials, particularly district coordinators, interfered with the decision-making process. Both the lack of independence of the courts and corruption weakened public confidence in the system and led to decisions that did not reflect what really happened during the genocide.

"Justice Compromised:
The Legacy of Rwanda's Community-Based Gacaca *Courts,"*
Human Rights Watch, 2011.

been too frightened to testify in defense of a Hutu man who had saved his life and those of more than a dozen of his relatives.

"A number of people told us they stayed silent during *Gacaca* trials even though they believed the suspects were innocent," Bekele said. "They felt the stakes were simply too high to come forward to defend people wrongly accused of genocide-related crimes."

Human Rights Watch also interviewed rape victims whose genocide-related cases were transferred in May 2008 from conventional courts, which have stronger privacy protection, to *Gacaca* courts, whose proceedings are known to the whole community, even if held behind closed doors. Many rape victims felt betrayed by this loss of confidentiality.

The government's decision to exclude crimes committed by soldiers of the current ruling party, the RPF, from *Gacaca* courts' jurisdiction has left victims of their crimes still waiting for justice, Human Rights Watch said. Soldiers of the RPF, which ended the genocide in July 1994 and went on to form the current government, killed tens of thousands of people between April and December 1994. In 2004, the *Gacaca* law was amended to exclude such crimes, and the government worked to ensure that these crimes were not discussed in *Gacaca*.

"One of the serious shortcomings of *Gacaca* has been its failure to provide justice to all victims of serious crimes committed in 1994," Bekele said. "By removing RPF crimes from their jurisdiction, the government limited the potential of the *Gacaca* courts to foster long-term reconciliation in Rwanda."

Serious miscarriages of justice should be reviewed by professional judges in specialized courts in the conventional system, rather than by *Gacaca* courts, as proposed by the Rwandan government in late 2010, Human Rights Watch said.

"If *Gacaca* courts review alleged miscarriages of justice, there is a risk of repeating some of the same problems," Bekele said. "Instead, the government should ensure the formal justice system reviews these cases in a professional, fair, and impartial way. This would help secure *Gacaca*'s legacy and strengthen Rwanda's justice system for generations to come."

Rwanda's "Genocidal Ideology" Law Is Too Restrictive

Amnesty International

Amnesty International (AI) is an international human rights organization. In the following viewpoint, AI urges Rwandan authorities to review and amend vague and sweeping laws meant to eliminate the "genocidal ideology" and "divisionism" that led to the 1994 genocide. As AI points out, these laws have been used in Rwanda by the ruling party to stifle freedom of speech, curb criticism of the government and its policies, and punish political enemies. As a result, Amnesty International maintains, journalists and political opponents have been imprisoned and even assassinated in the run-up to the 2010 elections.

As you read, consider the following questions:

1. As the report identifies, which political group is in power in Rwanda?

2. According to AI, how many Rwandans were killed in the 1994 genocide?

3. How many years in prison was editor Agnes Nkusi Uwimana sentenced to in 2011 after publishing op-ed pieces critical to the ruling party, according to AI?

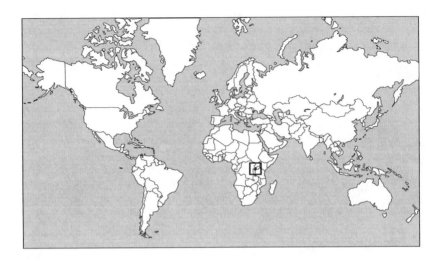

The Rwandan Patriotic Front (RPF), in power since the 1994 genocide, tightly controls political space, civil society and the media, contending that this is necessary to prevent renewed violence. Human rights defenders, journalists and political opponents cannot openly and publicly criticize the authorities. People who do speak out risk prosecution and imprisonment.

Restrictions on freedom of association and expression prevented new opposition parties from contesting the August 2010 elections. During this period, journalists were subjected to criminal sanctions for defamation. The Rwandan government did not respond constructively to criticism but rather tried to stamp it out.

Many Rwandans, even those with specialist knowledge of Rwandan law including lawyers and human rights workers, were unable to precisely define "genocide ideology."

Criminalizing Criticism

Vague and sweeping laws on "divisionism" and "genocide ideology" were introduced in Rwanda in the decade after the

1994 genocide. Up to 800,000 Rwandans were killed in the genocide, mostly ethnic Tutsi, but also Hutu who opposed the organized killing. The laws prohibit hate speech, but are broadly drafted so that they criminalize expression that does not amount to hate speech, including legitimate criticism of the government. The laws contravene Rwanda's regional and international human rights obligations and commitments to freedom of expression, and the vague wording is deliberately exploited to violate human rights.

In its August 2010 report, "Safer to Stay Silent: The Chilling Effect of Rwanda's Laws on 'Genocide Ideology' and 'Sectarianism,'" Amnesty International described how the vague wording of these laws is misused to criminalize criticism of the government and legitimate dissent by opposition politicians, human rights activists and journalists.

Amnesty International found that many Rwandans, even those with specialist knowledge of Rwandan law including lawyers and human rights workers, were unable to precisely define "genocide ideology". Even judges, the professionals charged with applying the law, noted that the law was broad and abstract.

At a local level, individuals appear to use "genocide ideology" accusations to settle personal disputes. These laws allow for the criminal punishment even of children under 12, as well as parents, guardians or teachers convicted of "inoculating" a child with "genocide ideology". Sentences for convicted adults range from 10 to 25 years' imprisonment.

Government Commitments to Legislative Reform

The Rwandan government expressed a commitment in April 2010 to review the "genocide ideology" law. During Rwanda's Universal Periodic Review at the UN [United Nations] Human Rights Council in January 2011, the Rwandan government reiterated this commitment and indicated that the 2009 media law, which unduly restricts freedom of expression, was also up for review.

Despite their recognition of the shortcomings of the "genocide ideology" law, the government continues to use it to prosecute individuals for legitimate criticism. It remains unclear whether the "divisionism" law, similarly used to silence critics, will also be revised. Since the elections, individuals have also been convicted of threatening state security, another charge carrying a heavy prison sentence, for criticizing the government.

The government clamped down on critics before the August 2010 presidential elections. They used regulatory sanctions, restrictive laws and criminal defamation cases to close down media outlets critical of the government.

The Rwandan Media High Council, a regulatory body close to the ruling party, suspended two private Kinyarwanda language newspapers, *Umuseso* and *Umuvugizi*, from April to October 2010. It then called for their indefinite closure, claiming that some of their articles threatened national security.

Jean-Bosco Gasasira, editor of *Umuvugizi*, and Didas Gasana, editor of *Umuseso*, fled Rwanda in April and May 2010 respectively after receiving threats.

An Opposition Politician Is Imprisoned

Rwandan opposition leader and founding president of the opposition Social Party [Imberakuri] (PS-Imberakuri), Bernard Ntaganda, was jailed on 11 February 2011 on politically motivated charges. He was sentenced to four years' imprisonment after being convicted of breaching state security, of "divisionism" for public speeches criticizing government policies ahead of the elections, and of attempting to plan an "unauthorized" demonstration. Bernard Ntaganda appealed against his conviction.

Bernard Ntaganda's conviction is part of a wider and concerning trend to prosecute individuals with threatening national security for legitimate criticism of the government. His prosecution for threatening state security and "divisionism" was based solely on his speeches criticizing government policies. The prosecution had requested a 10-year prison sentence for these two charges and contended that "paint[ing] a negative image of state authority" could cause the population to rebel and create unrest.

Bernard Ntaganda was arrested at dawn on 24 June 2010—the first day that presidential candidates could register for the elections—and just hours before a demonstration planned by his party in the capital, Kigali. Although Bernard Ntaganda had requested authorization to hold the demonstration, according to the prosecution the authorities had attempted to notify him that it was banned only on the day before it was due to take place. The defence said the demonstrators were unaware of the ban.

The Social Party [Imberakuri] (PS-Imberakuri) was the only new party which successfully secured registration. It was later infiltrated by dissident members who decided not to field a candidate in the elections.

Bernard Ntaganda was called before the Senate in late 2009 to respond to "genocide ideology" accusations. In April 2010, the Senate's political commission said they felt such accusations were well founded.

The government should immediately and unconditionally release Bernard Ntaganda, imprisoned for expressing his opinion without advocating violence.

Journalists Are Imprisoned

Agnes Nkusi Uwimana, editor of the private Kinyarwanda newspaper *Umurabyo*, and her deputy editor, Saidati Mukakibibi, were sentenced on 5 February 2011 to 17 and seven years in prison respectively for opinion pieces published before the elections. Both women appealed against their conviction.

Agnes Nkusi Uwimana was found guilty of threatening state security, "genocide ideology", "divisionism" and defamation, and Saidati Mukakibibi was found guilty of threatening state security. The two women were prosecuted over several articles in which they criticized government policies and made corruption allegations against senior government officials, including President [Paul] Kagame. The articles also made references to the prevailing feeling of insecurity before the elections and contended that there were growing divisions within the security forces.

Before prosecution, Agnes Nkusi Uwimana was called before the Rwandan Media High Council to respond to allegations that her articles were defamatory.

The government should immediately and unconditionally release Agnes Nkusi Uwimana and Saidati Mukakibibi, imprisoned for exercising their right to freedom of expression without advocating violence.

Journalist Is Murdered

Rwandan journalist and deputy editor of the Kinyarwanda newspaper *Umuvugizi*, Jean-Léonard Rugambage, was shot dead outside his home in Kigali at 10 p.m. on 24 June 2010. He was the first Rwandan journalist to be murdered in recent years.

Jean-Léonard Rugambage had been investigating the shooting in the same month of the exiled former head of the Rwandan army, Kayumba Nyamwasa, in South Africa. Earlier on 24 June, *Umuvugizi* had published an online article alleging that Rwandan intelligence officials were linked to the shooting. In the days before his murder, Jean-Léonard Rugambage told colleagues that he felt surveillance over him had intensified.

There is no evidence that Rwandan police have explored those leads into the killing of Jean-Léonard Rugambage that pointed towards it being politically motivated. Within days of the murder, two suspects were arrested. In October, they were convicted of the murder and sentenced to life imprisonment. They claimed that Jean-Léonard Rugambage had killed one of their family members during the 1994 genocide. A case had been brought against Jean-Léonard Rugambage on these same allegations in 2005 before a *Gacaca* court (community tribunals to expedite trials of the vast majority of people suspected of participation in the genocide) after he published an article critical of *Gacaca*. However, it was dropped for lack of evidence.

Amnesty International believes that the government should re-open the investigation (by establishing an independent commission of enquiry) into the killing of Jean-Léonard Rugambage with a view to investigating all possible leads.

An Opposition Politician Is Murdered

On 14 July 2010, André Kagwa Rwisereka, vice president of the opposition Democratic Green Party, was found dead in Butare, southern Rwanda. He had been beheaded.

André Kagwa Rwisereka, who left the RPF to create the Democratic Green Party, had told colleagues in the weeks before his murder that he was concerned for his security. Other Democratic Green Party members said they had also received threats.

No one has been brought to justice for André Kagwa Rwisereka's murder. The police opened investigations, but the prosecution claims to have insufficient evidence to press charges. Amnesty International calls on the government to establish an independent commission of inquiry into André Kagwa Rwisereka's death.

Cambodian Trials of Former Khmer Rouge Soldiers Stir Up Controversy

Sebastian Strangio

Sebastian Strangio is a correspondent for GlobalPost. In the following viewpoint, he reports that recent war crimes trials related to the genocide carried out by the Khmer Rouge in Cambodia in the late 1970s have been gripped by suspicion and fear. According to Strangio, many Cambodians are anxious that the trials will cast too wide a net and question the court's independence. At issue is the trial of an elderly man, Meas Muth, accused of horrible war crimes—but now defended by his neighbors as a gentle and wise man who is being unfairly treated. Survivors and families of victims worry that the war crimes tribunals will be shut down before justice is served, asserts Strangio.

As you read, consider the following questions:

1. According to the author, how many Cambodians were massacred by the Khmer Rouge between 1975 and 1979?
2. How many tons of munitions does the author say were used during the US bombing campaign of Cambodia?
3. What did Cambodian prime minister Hun Sen tell visiting UN secretary-general Ban Ki-Moon about the genocide trials in 2010, according to Strangio?

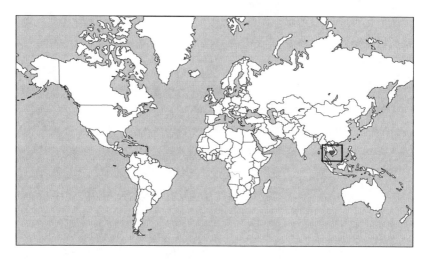

On June 27 [2011], at the war crimes tribunal in Cambodia's capital Phnom Penh, four former leaders of the Khmer Rouge [KR] regime will finally face the music.

More than three decades since the regime's fall, former KR foreign minister Ieng Sary, head of state Khieu Samphan and minister of social affairs Ieng Thirith, along with "Brother No. 2" Nuon Chea, are being tried on charges of genocide, war crimes and crimes against humanity for their role in the 1975–79 regime, which led to the death of an estimated 1.7 million Cambodians.

Coming on the heels of last year's [2010's] conviction of Kaing Guek Eav (alias Duch) for his role in the deaths of up to 16,000 people at Phnom Penh's notorious S-21 prison, the trial holds out the promise of justice long delayed.

A Different Perspective on the Genocide Trials

But hundreds of miles away in Ta Sanh Cheung, a small village along the Thai border, the trials have proven a tough sell. The hamlet lies in Samlot district in Cambodia's west, a former stronghold of the KR movement. Residents here, many of them former Communist fighters, say they are worried that the [United Nations] U.N.-backed tribunal will soon start to cast a wider net.

Tith Ron, a 59-year-old former KR soldier who joined the movement in the 1970s at the age of 19, defended the regime's actions, and criticized instead the American carpet bombing of Cambodia in the late 1960s and early 1970s.

"The Americans killed more Cambodian people more than Pol Pot did," he alleged, referring to the regime's "Brother No. 1," who died on the Thai border in 1998. The U.S. bombing of Cambodia devastated large swathes of the countryside and is estimated to have killed hundreds of thousands. It is estimated that more than 2 million tons of munitions were used during the campaign.

"If they want to sentence us they should also bring the Americans, because they dropped 7 million tons of B-52 [munitions] onto our heads. We were Cambodians saving Cambodians—how can they sentence us?" Tith asked.

Locals were particularly worried after recent radio broadcasts named an elderly local resident as a war crimes suspect in the tribunal's potential third case. The man named was Meas Muth, the former commander of the KR navy, who defected to the government in 1999 in return for a cushy military post and a peaceful retirement in Ta Sanh Cheung.

The US bombing of Cambodia devastated large swathes of the countryside and is estimated to have killed hundreds of thousands.

Along with Sou Met, the ex-head of the KR air force, leaked court documents accuse him of the torture, killing and the forced labor of tens of thousands of people under the regime. A 2001 paper by historian Stephen Heder and legal expert Brian Tittemore said the pair played a direct role in the arrest and transfer of purged cadres to S-21 prison, where many were subsequently tortured and killed.

Meas Muth's home stands at a quiet end of Ta Sanh Cheung village, a three-story wooden structure topped with satellite dishes. On a recent Saturday, he was asleep in a hammock strung up over a wooden platform outside his home, his mouth hanging open and one leg dangling over the side. A book of Buddhist parables lay on a nearby chair, a slip of paper marking the page. Discarded skins of the rambutan fruit lay in a pile on the planks below.

A New Man?

Since his KR days, Meas Muth—now a hunched man with thinning, ash-grey hair—has reinvented himself as something of a Buddhist patriarch, bankrolling the construction of a new pagoda in the village and showering local villagers with sagely aphorisms. ("If you give someone happiness other people will give you happiness back," he said). It is a strange—maybe cynical—turn for a senior member of a regime that banned religion and put tens of thousands of Buddhist monks to work in massive labor camps.

However, Meas Muth flatly denied any involvement in mass atrocities, saying his responsibility was to protect the country's coast from foreign invasion. "I was a lower officer who was willing to protect Cambodia's independence and neutrality, and prevent Cambodia from being controlled by foreigners. I was not a Khmer Rouge leader," Meas Muth said, fashioning home-grown tobacco into a stubby facsimile of a cigarette.

"If I did bad I couldn't sleep here in a hammock. Somebody might throw a stone at me or sometime might take a knife and kill me. But I am living in safety." Despite being banned by the KR, he added, Buddhism continued to live on "in his mind" under the regime.

Overview of the Khmer Rouge

The Communist Party of Kampuchea (CPK), otherwise known as the Khmer Rouge, took control of Cambodia on April 17, 1975. The CPK created the state of Democratic Kampuchea in 1976 and ruled the country until January 1979. The party's existence was kept secret until 1977, and no one outside the CPK knew who its leaders were (the leaders called themselves "Angkar Padevat").

While the Khmer Rouge was in power, they set up policies that disregarded human life and produced repression and massacres on a massive scale. They turned the country into a huge detention center, which later became a graveyard for nearly two million people, including their own members and even some senior leaders.

"Historical Overview of the Khmer Rouge,"
Cambodia Tribunal Monitor, 2011.

Locals described the accused war criminal as a "good Buddhist" and a patriot who pedals advice about everything from farming and business to spiritual matters. Another former KR soldier, Toch Pha, 54, said villagers were angered by the accusations against him. He said, "If they come to arrest him we will not allow them to take him out of the village."

The Courts Inspire Fear and Suspicion

But whatever the evidence against him, Meas Muth will probably never see the inside of a courtroom. In recent months, the tribunal—known officially as the Extraordinary Chambers in the Courts of Cambodia (ECCC)—has been plagued by suspicions, internal rifts and a flurry of resignations over the issue of whether to pursue the case against Meas Muth and Sou Met.

Critics have accused judges of moving to quash the case, known as Case 003, which has long been opposed by Cambodian Prime Minister Hun Sen, who last year [2010] told visiting U.N. Secretary-General Ban Ki-moon that indictments beyond the current case were "not allowed." Observers say Cambodian judges on the hybrid court have parroted Hun Sen's line, calling into question the court's independence.

The issue came to a head in April when the ECCC's two co-investigating judges—You Bunleng of Cambodia and Siegfried Blunk of Germany—announced the hasty completion of their investigation into Case 003. Critics say the judges conducted a perfunctory probe as a prelude to burying the case.

"The judges have a duty—it's not an option—to investigate," said Theary Seng, a human rights activist and victims advocate. "They have failed in their duty to investigate and they have failed to inform the public." The co-investigating judges have also remained silent about Case 004, a further case involving three mid-ranking KR officials.

Escaping Justice

The tribunal's credibility continues to ebb. Four Western legal staff from the investigating judges' office have reportedly resigned over the handling of Case 003, with one of them describing the atmosphere in the office as "toxic." There have also been calls for an official U.N. investigation into political interference at the court.

Though Geneva has rejected the call, asserting the ECCC's continued independence, observers say the court's credibility is on the line.

"It could be incredibly significant," Anne Heindel, a legal adviser for the Documentation Center of Cambodia, which researches Khmer Rouge history, said of the Case 003 controversy. "If the court is seen as not fulfilling its procedure—as not adhering to the rules—then it will taint the entire process, including Case 001 and Case 002. There's no way you can separate Case 003 out from what's come before."

While Hun Sen may squash the possibility of further trials, Theary Seng, who blames Meas Muth for the death of her own parents during the Pol Pot regime, said such an outcome would compromise the current case and deepen the cynicism of ordinary Cambodians.

"It's not surprising he should deny his role, but he can't deny the weight of evidence. He can't deny the testimonies that run into the tens of thousands," she said of Meas Muth. "There's no magic number as to how many should be prosecuted and should be indicted. But the current five are not sufficient for the crimes that took the lives of 1.7 million Cambodians."

Iran Must Face the Consequences of Its Attempts to Incite Genocide

Irwin Cotler

Irwin Cotler is a Canadian member of Parliament and former justice minister. In the following viewpoint, he criticizes the international community for virtually ignoring the hateful rhetoric on Israel spewed by Iranian leaders such as Mahmoud Ahmadinejad. Cotler maintains that Iran's calls to wipe Israel off the map as well as other threats amount to an incitement to genocide, which is prohibited under the genocide convention of the United Nations. Therefore, Iran should be called to account and face the consequences for its actions, Cotler concludes.

As you read, consider the following questions:

1. What does the author say is "the enduring lesson of the Holocaust and of the genocides in Srebrenica, Rwanda and Darfur"?
2. What head of state does the author say was convicted for incitement to genocide?
3. According to Cotler, what did former Iranian president Akbar Hashemi Rafsanjani say about Israel?

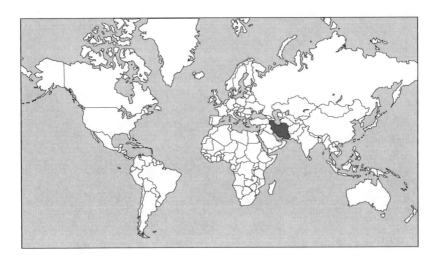

The enduring lesson of the Holocaust and of the genocides in Srebrenica, Rwanda and Darfur is that they occurred not simply because of the machinery of death but because of the state-sanctioned incitement to hate and genocide. This teaching of contempt, this demonisation of the other, is where it all begins.

Limits on Free Speech

There is no such thing as the absolute protection of free speech. All constitutional democracies exclude some categories of speech from protection, be it obscenity, fighting words or racist hate speech.

One must not wait until after the genocide. One must act to prevent it by prohibiting the incitement.

Yet even if one were to argue against any hate speech law, even if one were to hold that the answer—and this is true—to hate speech is more speech, there is still a fundamental difference between hate speech in a constitutional democracy, and state-sanctioned incitement to genocide in a non-democracy such as Iran.

The United Nations [UN] genocide convention prohibits the direct and public incitement to genocide. It is prohibited under principles and precedents from Nuremberg to the International Criminal Tribunal for the former Yugoslavia and Rwanda. Those cases held that even a head of state, such as the former [prime minister] of Rwanda, Jean Kambanda, could be convicted for incitement to genocide.

One must not wait until after the genocide. One must act to prevent it by prohibiting the incitement.

A Major Threat

We face an emerging threat from [President] Mahmoud Ahmadinejad's Iran. What distinguishes Iran from the Holocaust, the former Yugoslavia and Rwanda is that in those the genocide had already occurred, and occurred because of state-sanctioned incitement to genocide. But in Ahmadinejad's Iran, the incitement to genocide—but not yet the genocide—has occurred. Therefore, the obligation to prevent and prohibit is compelling.

We are witnessing the toxic convergence of the advocacy of the most horrific of crimes, genocide, embedded in the most virulent of hatreds, anti-Semitism. It is dramatised by the parading in [Iran's capital] Tehran streets of a Shahab-3 missile draped in the words "Israel must be wiped off the map" while the assembled thousands are exhorted to chants of "death to Israel".

Ahmadinejad's Iran is increasingly resorting to incendiary and demonising language, including epidemiological metaphors reminiscent of Nazi incitement. Ahmadinejad and other officials characterise Israel as a "filthy germ", a "stain of disgrace" and "a stinking corpse", while referring to Israelis as "the true manifestation of Satan" and "blood-thirsty barbarians", as a prologue to—and justification for—a Middle East genocide, while at the same time denying the Nazi one.

"Ahmadinejad and the Holocaust," cartoon by Alex Faffi, www.CartoonStockcom. Copyright © Alex Faffi. Reproduction rights obtainable from www.CartoonStock.com.

The Dangerous Rhetoric of Iran

Calls by senior figures in the Iranian leadership for the destruction of Israel are frighteningly reminiscent of calls for the Rwandan extermination of Tutsis by the Hutu leadership. The crucial difference is that the Hutus were equipped with machetes, while Iran, in defiance of the world community, continues its pursuit of the most destructive of weaponry: nuclear arms.

Iran has developed and tested a long-range missile delivery system for that purpose, while former president Akbar Hashemi Rafsanjani asserts that "the employment of even one atomic bomb inside Israel will wipe it off the face of the earth".

In the face of this hateful and inciting context, the international community has responded with silence verging on active acquiescence. That Ahmadinejad was invited to address the General Assembly of the UN—or even the Durban Review

Conference in Geneva, supposedly on the topic of combating racism, on the day of Holocaust remembrance—thus giving him an international stage to further spread his message of hatred, is a mockery of history, law and the UN itself.

The precedents of the international criminal tribunals ought to be applied: An individual who incites to genocide, who pursues the most destructive of weaponry in violation of UN Security Council resolutions, who is complicit in crimes against humanity through genocidal terrorist proxies, who warns Muslims who support Israel that they will "burn in the fire of the Islamic umma", who is engaged in a massive repression of human rights in Iran, and who assaults the basic tenet of the UN charter, belongs in the dock of the accused, rather than before a UN podium.

Canada Should Support the UN in Preventing Mass Violence

Lloyd Axworthy and Allan Rock

Lloyd Axworthy is president of the University of Winnipeg and a former Canadian foreign minister. Allan Rock is president of the University of Ottawa and a former special advisor to the United Nations on Sri Lanka. In the following viewpoint, they assess the successes and failures of the United Nations Responsibility to Protect (R2P) doctrine, which obliges the international community to act more aggressively to protect people from mass violence and genocide. Axworthy and Rock urge Canada to support the R2P doctrine, arguing that the nation has a unique and important opportunity to champion the ideals of R2P and ensure that the doctrine is used fairly and properly.

As you read, consider the following questions:

1. When do the authors say that the UN took action against violence with R2P?
2. According to the authors, what happened at a 2009 debate in the UN General Assembly on R2P?
3. How do the authors think that R2P should have been used to better address the violence in Darfur?

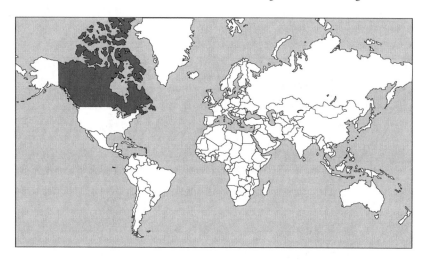

Five years ago this week [September 2005], with the horrors of Rwanda and Srebrenica still vivid in memory, the members of the United Nations [UN] vowed to take collective action, including military force if necessary, to prevent or stop mass violence within a state when the national government is unable or unwilling to do so.

The UN's unanimous endorsement of the doctrine of Responsibility to Protect (R2P) changed forever the Westphalian model of state sovereignty. For the first time, an exception was made to the UN charter's prohibition against international involvement in members' domestic jurisdiction. Lawful external action may now interfere with the conduct of sovereign rulers within their own states, albeit in obvious cases when they are killing their own people en masse.

Assessing R2P

As former political practitioners who respectively played a role in the conception of R2P (through the establishment of the International Commission on Intervention and State Sovereignty) and then its adoption (by leading the Canadian advocacy and negotiation efforts at the 2005 UN World Summit in New York), we find after five years reason for both encouragement and disappointment.

On the positive side, R2P is increasingly secure as an emerging norm of international conduct. It has been reaffirmed by the UN Security Council in responding to protection issues. The secretary-general has created in-house mechanisms to institutionalize it. Best of all, a 2009 debate in the General Assembly that might have risked a repeal turned instead into an overwhelming confirmation of its value.

On the other hand, R2P has failed to fulfill its promise in places such as Darfur and the Democratic Republic of the Congo. Theoretical advances are of no comfort to defenceless civilians savaged by lawless militias or wicked regimes. Even R2P's most ardent advocates have asked whether anything has really changed. Why didn't this breakthrough save civilian populations whose own governments were unable or unwilling to protect them?

Outstanding Issues

We suggest that there are two related issues to be addressed before R2P can move fully from paper to practice.

First, resort to R2P has been timid and halting. In Darfur, it should have been the fulcrum to leverage wider condemnation of the Khartoum regime. Early and vigorous shunning might have halted the state-sponsored violence. In the Congo, the sexual devastation of vast numbers of women by roving criminals is an atrocity needing an international response because the national government is incapable of protecting them. In such clear cases, we should lose our shyness about invoking R2P. Timely and concerted action—even well short of military intervention (the very last resort)—can save lives.

Second, the R2P "toolbox" must be filled with items needed to make the concept operational. The early-warning system agreed to in 2005 has yet to be put in place. R2P still lacks a gender dimension for the protection of women and girls, demonstrated dramatically by the systematic rape of

The Responsibility to Protect (R2P) Doctrine

Each individual State has the responsibility to protect its populations from genocide, war crimes, ethnic cleansing and crimes against humanity. This responsibility entails the prevention of such crimes, including their incitement, through appropriate and necessary means. . . . The international community should, as appropriate, encourage and help States to exercise this responsibility and support the United Nations in establishing an early-warning capability.

The international community, through the United Nations, also has the responsibility to use appropriate diplomatic, humanitarian and other peaceful means . . . to help protect populations from genocide, war crimes, ethnic cleansing and crimes against humanity. In this context, we are prepared to take collective action . . . on a case-by-case basis and in cooperation with relevant regional organizations as appropriate, should peaceful means be inadequate and national authorities manifestly fail to protect their populations from genocide, war crimes, ethnic cleansing and crimes against humanity. We stress the need for the General Assembly to continue consideration of the responsibility to protect populations from genocide, war crimes, ethnic cleansing and crimes against humanity and its implications, bearing in mind the principles of the Charter and international law. We also intend to commit ourselves, as necessary and appropriate, to helping States build capacity to protect their populations from genocide, war crimes, ethnic cleansing and crimes against humanity and to assisting those which are under stress before crises and conflicts break out.

World Summit Outcome Document, UN General Assembly,
September 2005.

hundreds of females in the Congo this summer [2010] and the abject failure of UN peacekeepers to protect them.

Above all, R2P needs a champion, a role that Canada once played.

Unfinished Business

Other items of unfinished business include:

- A wider range of targeted sanctions with maximum impact on a rogue regime. More creative thought is needed to develop population-friendly, regime-punishing, pressure-producing, readily enforceable and truly effective sanctions.

- Trained mediators for early deployment to ensure that violence doesn't spiral into mass atrocity. [Former UN secretary-general] Kofi Annan's intervention in Kenya is a textbook example of R2P at work, preventing the post-election violence from becoming an all-out ethnic bloodbath. Our capacity for such activist diplomacy must be built up.

- A standing rapid-response force with specialized training and equipment, so that protection is only a few hours away when the Security Council authorizes protection. The current practice of cobbling a force together from many contributing countries takes months and produces an uncoordinated team with uneven preparation.

Canada's Role in R2P

Above all, R2P needs a champion, a role that Canada once played. If we win election to the Security Council next month [October 2010], our country should rediscover this important cause.

In 2007, Sir Martin Gilbert, a historian and [former British prime minister] Winston Churchill's official biographer, asserted in these pages: "Since the Peace of Westphalia in 1648, non-interference in the internal policies even of the most repressive governments was the golden rule of international diplomacy. The Canadian-sponsored concept of 'responsibility to protect' proposed the most significant adjustment to national sovereignty in 360 years."

By advocating R2P in appropriate cases and fashioning tools to make it effective, Canada can ensure that humanity makes the most of this historic breakthrough.

Periodical and Internet Sources Bibliography

The following articles have been selected to supplement the diverse views presented in this chapter.

Simon Allison	"U.S. Troops Hunt Al Qaeda on Continent, Not LRA," *Daily Maverick*, October 17, 2011. http://dailymaverick.co.za.
Stephen L. Carter	"America's Risky New Path," Daily Beast, March 28, 2011. www.thedailybeast.com.
Daniel R. DePetris	"Fighting a Terror Kingpin in Africa," *Global Public Square* (blog), October 17, 2011. http://globalpublicsquare.blogs.cnn.com.
Tim Gallimore	"An Unfair Target for Criticism," *Independent* (Kampala), October 5, 2011.
Ann Garrison	"Rwanda's Packed Prisons and Genocide Ideology Law," *San Francisco Bay View*, April 7, 2010.
James A. Goldston	"Justice Delayed and Denied," *New York Times*, October 13, 2011.
Daniel Howden	"Genocide Courts Attacked for Failure to Heal Rwanda's Scars," *Independent* (UK), August 5, 2011.
Peter Maguire	"Cambodia and the Pitfalls of Political Justice," *New York Times*, June 20, 2011.
John Pilger	"The Son of Africa Claims a Continent's Crown Jewels," *New Statesman*, October 20, 2011.
Paul R. Pillar	"A Humanitarian Intervention Worth Doing," *National Interest*, October 16, 2011.

GLOBALVIEWPOINTS

The Legacy of Genocide

Rwanda Is Moving Forward from the 1994 Genocide

Kevin Whitelaw

Kevin Whitelaw is the deputy assistant managing editor for US News & World Report. *In the following viewpoint, he examines Rwanda's progress since the 1994 genocide, particularly its attempts to confront its legacy and impart a lasting reconciliation between the Hutus and Tutsis. For many, Whitelaw asserts, it has been a very difficult process—survivors are often forced to interact with those who perpetrated the violence or stood by while innocent people were massacred. Whitelaw points out that despite these challenges, the tiny African country has emerged as a surprising success story.*

As you read, consider the following questions:

1. Why were eight thousand Rwandan genocide suspects released in February 2007, according to the author?
2. What did one Rwandan journalist call the regime of President Paul Kagame?
3. According to the author, what percentage of Rwandans have been born since the 1994 genocide?

Ezekiel Nzamwita fidgets awkwardly in a ratty T-shirt and baggy jacket. The onetime primary-school teacher is still getting used to civilian garb after spending a decade in prison-

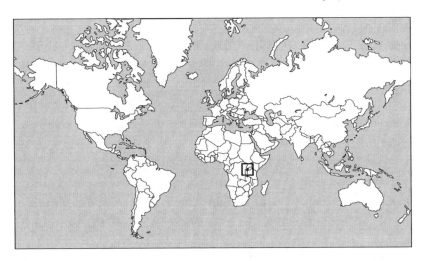

issue pink jumpsuits. "Ten years is a long time," he says, "but things have become better." A confessed killer, Nzamwita is one of about 8,000 genocide suspects released in February from Rwanda's overcrowded prisons as part of a national reconciliation effort after the 1994 bloodletting that claimed a million lives. The 51-year-old Hutu admitted being part of a group that killed a Tutsi man and stole his cows. Nzamwita won his freedom after asking the victim's brother for forgiveness.

He has spent the past few weeks at a "solidarity camp" run by the government. The camp is part of a massive effort to help reintegrate former prisoners, returning rebel soldiers, and longtime refugees into the new Rwanda. Before being released, Nzamwita must sit through a month of lectures on subjects ranging from Rwandan history and the government's political philosophy to the current banking system and new national health insurance scheme. "I think Rwanda will be a correct society now," Nzamwita says, only days away from his full release. "Even in prison, people regret that they were involved in the genocide."

Walking around the capital of Kigali, it is possible, at least for a moment, to forget that only 13 years ago, this tidy city

was littered with corpses from one of the most brutal genocides the world has seen. Now, the same streets are scrubbed
clean and the gutters are painstakingly weeded. "What's surprising here," says U.S. Ambassador to Rwanda Michael Arietti, "is that this place works at all." Indeed, it is, by some
measures, thriving. Modern office buildings and gleaming
shopping malls now dominate the center of town. New pros-
perous suburban developments look distinctly European, with
their red-tile roofs and bountiful gardens. (Not everything
works—the city's 10 traffic lights have been dark for months.)
In fact, Kigali has now become one of the safest, most func-
tional cities in Africa—particularly in comparison with its
troubled neighbors, whether it's lawless Congo to the west or
the crime-infested Kenyan capital of Nairobi to the east.

---

*It is not at all clear that Rwanda can truly escape that
legacy of genocide.*

While Rwanda might not yet be the Switzerland of East
Africa, its government has charted a surprisingly ambitious
course for this tiny and startlingly green country known as
the Land of a Thousand Hills. The goal is to become a regional stronghold for communications and computing, a place
where ethnic divisions like Hutu and Tutsi are a thing of the
past. Fiber-optic cable is being laid throughout the country,
and Rwanda soon will have perhaps the most advanced broadband wireless Internet network on the continent. "We will be
the nervous system for the region," says Romain Murenzi, the
country's minister for science and technology. While it still
has a very long way to go, Rwanda's broad-based government
is winning praise from foreign governments and aid groups
alike for its good intentions and surprising lack of corruption.
It has doubled primary-school enrollment in the past decade
and has established a national health insurance system. "They
are," says Arietti, "doing all the right things."

Fear. But the painful memories of the three-month frenzy of mass killing—one that swept up almost the entire nation as either victims or killers, witnesses or collaborators—lurk everywhere just below the nation's placid surface. And it is not at all clear that Rwanda can truly escape that legacy of genocide. Survivors have been brutally assaulted—many fatally—in a series of isolated but steady attacks in recent years. Privately, many Tutsis admit that they cannot shake the feeling that it is only the government's sometimes-suffocating control over dialogue and events in the country that prevents Hutu extremists from killing again. "I fear that, inside, they are not satisfied," whispers one Tutsi.

This was a particularly ugly slice of history. The Hutu government of the time orchestrated and incited the attacks on the minority Tutsi. But they were carried out largely by the people themselves. The killing was intensely personal; the machete was the weapon of choice. Farmers killed their neighbors. Doctors killed other doctors. Students killed their fellow students. Even some priests helped to kill large swaths of their congregations. Later, there were reprisal killings. Rwanda is now struggling to answer a very tough question: Is reconciliation truly possible in the wake of such barbarity?

Imakulata Mukankundiye is emblematic of both Rwanda's past and its future. The 50-year-old widow's tiny farm in southern Rwanda produces some of the finest coffee in the world. As part of the Maraba coffee cooperative, she has been at the vanguard of Rwanda's entry into the gourmet coffee market, where her beans command high prices from roasters in America and Britain. Even with only 250 coffee trees, she makes enough to live on these days. The mud walls of her cramped, dirt-floored home are painted white, and a radio in the yard runs off a small solar-powered battery.

Before the genocide, she worked on her farm with her husband and six children. One Friday morning in the spring of 1994, several of her neighbors stormed onto her farm, pulled the family out into the yard, and burned down her house. After cutting the throats of her cows, they dragged away her Tutsi husband and four of her children. Being Hutu, she was spared, along with her two daughters. The males were taken to a Roman Catholic church, where they remained for several days with little food or water. "We knew they would be killed," she says. On the fourth day, the Hutu militia men threw grenades into the church and finished off the survivors with machetes and spears. In all, she lost 17 family members that day.

Today, her older daughter works as a tailor, and the younger one is in school. Several of the men who came to her farm that fateful morning confessed to their crimes and live again in the village freely. "No one came to me directly and apologized," she says. "Never." Yet some of them have since returned to her farm, this time seeking work. "I lost the rest of my family, so I have to hire them," she says. "Inside me, I am not comfortable, but the government asked us for reconciliation and to forgive them. I don't have a choice." After all, someone has to bring in the harvest.

The healing process is understandably painful and slow— and aggravated by the glacial pace of justice.

Other Rwandans have found it even more difficult. One Tutsi man lost both of his parents and seven of his nine brothers and sisters. Recently, he confronted one of his father's killers in prison, asking how he could have killed the man who helped pay his children's school fees. The prisoner replied only, "Because he was a Tutsi." There was no apology or regret. Now, he struggles with how to answer when his children ask why they don't have any grandparents. They need to know the truth, he says, but "I don't want them to feel hatred for Hutus."

Still, apart from the isolated incidents of violence, the Rwandan government has largely kept a lid on tension, mainly by exercising tight control over the nation's dialogue. One Rwandan journalist terms the regime of President Paul Kagame "a progressive dictatorship." The aim is an idealistic one—creating a single nation without ethnic splits. "We think the way to heal the divide and heal Rwanda is to promote Rwandan identity above other identities," explains Fatuma Ndangiza, who heads the National Unity and Reconciliation Commission. "We're saying Rwanda first, Hutu and Tutsi later." While Rwanda is technically a multiparty state, politics are still regulated. The ruling party cannot hold more than half of the cabinet posts, but all political parties must be members of the unity government, and decisions are made by consensus. Politicians debate almost exclusively behind closed doors, meaning there is little discussion in public. "We have a society that is deeply divided," says Tito Rutaremara, the government's ombudsman. "Is it good to create a democracy based on division or a democracy based on consensus? The people told us politicians to reconcile ourselves before coming to them."

But growing numbers of Rwandans are complaining about the government's occasional heavy-handedness. Open discussion of ethnic differences is punished, and many independent journalists report having violent run-ins with the authorities. "If someone talks about Hutu or Tutsi, he is branded a divider," says Didas Gasana, editor of *Newsline*, an independent English-language weekly newspaper. "But this is something we have to face up to. . . . When you try to suppress people's feelings and opinions, the time will come when there will be an explosion." Some Rwandan officials concede that they will have to gradually loosen the reins but say it's a difficult balancing act.

The healing process is understandably painful and slow—and aggravated by the glacial pace of justice. With nearly 90,000 genocide suspects in jail, many without trials, Rwanda's damaged courts (and even the United Nations war-crimes tribunal) are simply incapable of handling the workload. In all, more than 750,000 cases (ranging from looting to murder) have yet to be tried anywhere. The country's answer has been to adapt a form of traditional justice, called *Gacaca*, to handle genocide cases. Judges are appointed by each local community, and attendance is mandatory for the entire village. While imperfect, the *Gacaca* process has allowed some measure of truth-telling for survivors to learn what happened to their relatives. "For some, it's really the first time they have talked about it since 1994," says Hugo Jombwe Moudiki, a Cameroonian who until last month ran the Rwanda office of Avocats Sans Frontières, an international legal group that monitors the *Gacaca* process. "But victims often think they don't get the whole truth, and the accused think it's rigged against them." The process is scheduled to wrap up at the end of this year, an impossible feat given that only 60,000 cases have been tried. The pace has picked up in recent months, but there is pressure to move even faster. "It's taking too much time," says Rutaremara, the ombudsman. "We need to focus on other problems."

In a recent daylong *Gacaca* session under a hot sun in the village of Nyamiyaga, the judges struggle to get through a dozen different cases, all involving murder charges. The entire village has turned out, gathering under a small cluster of trees. The easiest cases are the full confessions, such as the one by Jean Nzabanita, who admits being part of a group that killed neighbors and stuffed their corpses into septic tanks. "We buried them like dogs," he tells the rapt audience. "During the genocide, we became like mad animals, and we lost our humanity. I think often that we would have been capable of anything." Relatives of his victims take their turn to stand up and confront him, demanding the truth. Under questioning from his neighbors, he reluctantly admits to attending meetings to plan who, exactly, would be killed.

Tangled cases. But most cases are far more complicated for these amateur courts. Louis Ngaruriye, a former mayor of the village, is pleading guilty to murder charges, but at the same time he denies participating in the genocide. "I didn't kill myself, but I was in the group of killers, and I didn't protect anyone," he says, prompting scornful laughs from villagers. Several witnesses come forward to testify that Ngaruriye was in charge of village security during the genocide and ran the roadblocks erected around the village to search for Tutsis. He continues to deny the accusations, but the judges still find him guilty. His case now awaits an appeal, but villagers were dissatisfied by the outcome. "During the genocide, they killed people with pleasure," scoffs one observer. "Now, they try to make themselves out to be angels."

If reconciliation is the biggest obstacle facing Rwanda, almost as serious is Rwanda's deep poverty. Nearly 90 percent of Rwandans live off subsistence farming, and the country's rural areas remain largely untouched by development. The bulk of people are subsistence farmers, cultivating every possible tiny plot of land in one of the most densely populated countries in the world. Annual per capita income is a paltry $230, well below the poverty level. "With the people we work with at CARE, I don't feel like I see a change in their purchasing power and economic situation," says Delphine Pinault, a health adviser in Rwanda for the international aid group. "There is no money circulating in the rural areas."

There are some encouraging exceptions, particularly in the coffee sector, Rwanda's most important export. "You could not create a more perfect environment for producing high-quality coffee," says Timothy Schilling, an agronomist from Texas A&M University who runs SPREAD, a project funded by the U.S. Agency for International Development to improve coffee cultivation and other crops. "Rwanda offers more attention and TLC per coffee plant than anyone else in the world." The average farmer cares for as few as 150 trees, compared with

Women and the 1994 Genocide

The 1994 genocide had terrible consequences on the people of Rwanda and the society as a whole. Besides the loss of one million people in a period of three months, a destroyed economy, millions fleeing into exile with many of them being taken as hostages by the ex-FAR (former Rwandan government forces) and the Interahamwe (militia who participated in the genocide), and over 120,000 persons detained in jails with very poor legal infrastructure and limited human resources, the Rwandan genocide shattered the dense local friendship networks and community solidarity that had traditionally provided solace and support for women. Particularly dispensing speedy and fair trials to the thousands of suspects of 1994 genocide and rendering justice to the families of survivors will contribute to break the culture of impunity.

There are thousands of women who are victims of rape, trauma, physical injuries, and above all social trust has dissolved. Abject poverty is still high and it is affecting mainly women from the rural areas. High rates of HIV/AIDS where more than 250,000 women were raped, sixty-six percent of women who were raped tested positive and other infectious diseases coupled with limited health facilities remain high. This situation had an impact not only on the mental health of women but also their physical well-being. Most of the survivors of the genocide, the majority of whom happen to be women, experience serious economic deprivation. The level of mistrust among the families of those who survived the genocide and those whose relatives are suspected to have committed genocide is still high and deep rooted.

John Mutamba and Jeanne Izabiliza,
"The Role of Women in Reconciliation and
Peace Building in Rwanda: Ten Years After Genocide, 1994–2004,"
National Unity and Reconciliation Commission, May 2005.

thousands in coffee powerhouses like Nicaragua. Despite its fertile soil, plentiful sunshine, and high-altitude climate, Rwanda was not a player in the high-end coffee world until very recently. In his seven years in Rwanda, Schilling has helped some 60,000 farms join the gourmet coffee market, taking sales from nothing in 2001 to nearly $4 million last year, in large part by standardizing the processing of the raw coffee cherries. Customers today include Starbucks and a variety of smaller U.S. roasters. Now the government hopes to do the same for the country's well-regarded but antiquated tea industry. Rwanda is also eyeing the market for essential oils for perfumes and aromatherapy.

The other bright spot has been tourism and Rwanda's famous mountain gorillas. More than 12,000 tourists (including nearly 4,000 Americans) made the trek last year to see the endangered primates. But there is limited room for growth. The number of visits is sharply restricted for conservation purposes (only eight visitors per day for each of the seven gorilla families). Instead, Rwanda is trying to bill itself as a luxury destination to attract tourists willing to spend $200 a day for a weeklong stay. The government is working now to market its other attractions, including Africa's last high-altitude national forest.

And then there's the high-tech sector. For now, Rwanda has focused on getting the basic infrastructure in place, including miles of fiber-optic cable. By the end of June, Rwanda will have broadband wireless Internet access nationwide, thanks to Terracom, an American-led company. Christopher Lundh, an American who is the company's recently arrived CEO, says Rwanda is very different from other African countries. "The one thing I have not run into here, at all, is corruption." Yet Rwanda can still be a frustrating environment for companies, as well as aid groups, to operate in. While the national leadership is well stocked with experienced technocrats, local leaders are more of a mixed bag. "Are there enough capable managers in this country to make things happen?" asks Josh Ruxin, a health expert at Columbia University who runs a development project in eastern Rwanda. "That will remain one of the top challenges in this country for some time to come."

The landlocked country has also never had much of an industrial base, and it has not yet been able to persuade major foreign investors to plunge into the Rwandan market. In part because of its ugly past, Rwanda has no shortage of high-profile visitors, from Microsoft's Bill Gates to Google executives. But that has not yet translated into an economic vote of confidence. "You haven't really had a major investment in Rwanda," says Arietti, the U.S. ambassador, "and that's what you need—a demonstration that there is the possibility of a big commercial success here."

Unfortunately, any progress could easily be overwhelmed by Rwanda's runaway population growth. The traditionally Roman Catholic country has been slow to face up to the need to reduce its family size. "Rwanda won't get anywhere with a birthrate of 6.1 [children] per woman," says Christophe Tocco, the acting director for the USAID [U.S. Agency for International Developmement] mission in Rwanda. President Kagame has started talking about the problem in public, but solutions have been slow.

Still, Rwanda does get high marks for its investment in the next generation. One of the largest and most modern buildings in the country is the new Kigali Institute of Science and Technology, which aims to enlarge Rwanda's nascent science and engineering community. About one-quarter of Rwandans are currently enrolled in primary or secondary schools. Rwanda has signed up for a program that promises to deliver one $100 laptop computer per child in the next five years, while most secondary schools already have at least 10 computers and Internet connectivity. Murenzi, the science and technology minister, says the key for the future is to develop the skills for critical thinking among Rwanda's youth. "During the genocide, critical thinking was absent," he says. "With access to the Internet, these kids will develop critical thinking. You bet on those who will be your workforce in 2020."

Rwanda's government also has been surprisingly successful at freeing the schools and government hiring practices from discrimination and preferential treatment, both hallmarks of pre-genocide Rwanda. But changing the perception among the people is more difficult, particularly with the government's enforced culture of silence about ethnicity. One Hutu aid worker talks about his struggle to register a new nonprofit group. His friends in exile warned him that the Tutsi-led government would never give him the correct permits. And indeed, his application was denied. "My first reaction could have been that they rejected me because I am a Hutu," he says. "But I talked to a Tutsi who had the same problems." While he says he now blames the cumbersome and frequently inept bureaucracy, "other Hutus might see this as discrimination." The government refuses to divulge any statistics on ethnicity, making it even more difficult to refute any suspicions among the Hutu majority.

New generation. There is still hope, of course, for the next generation. About 45 percent of Rwandans have been born since the genocide. But Yvonne Kayiteshonga, who runs the mental health department at the health ministry, worries that this generation is already being scarred by the past. Her counselors have seen it in school, as well as in the psychiatric clinics. "Children as young as 8 cannot follow their studies," she says. "The trauma of the parents is being passed on to their children. We see it every day." The toughest time for everybody is the month of April, during the annual commemoration of the genocide.

Some young Rwandans are banding together. Marguerite Mukasine is a 22-year-old coffee farmer in the village of Nyakizu in southern Rwanda. She belongs to a local group called

Jyambere Rubyirnko, or Lift Up Youth, along with 29 other young men and women. The group jointly contributes to a bank account, which is available for loans when a member needs help. A genocide survivor, Mukasine lost two brothers and a sister in 1994. One of the killers came to her parents to ask for forgiveness, which they granted. "So I think it's normal to accept," she says. "For others, I don't know." In her youth group, they meet once a month to discuss everything from AIDS to reconciliation. The members, who include both survivors and children of parents in prison for genocide crimes, also discuss their stories from the genocide. "Nobody," she says, "has a happy story." Still, she brims with hope for the future. "It will not happen again," she says. "We are stopping the mistakes of our parents."

The Rwanda Genocide Led to More Aggressive International Justice Efforts

Scott Baldauf

Scott Baldauf is a staff writer for the Christian Science Monitor. *In the following viewpoint, he finds that one of the most important legacies of the 1994 Rwandan genocide is the international community's commitment to more aggressive and comprehensive efforts to deal with rogue regimes and stop genocidal campaigns. Baldauf maintains that international justice efforts by institutions like the International Criminal Court have become proactive in trying to protect vulnerable populations and save lives. This change can be felt in war zones like Darfur and the Democratic Republic of the Congo, Baldauf asserts.*

As you read, consider the following questions:

1. How long does the author say that the Rwandan massacre lasted?

2. According to the author, what Congolese warlord was arrested and will be tried for war crimes?

3. On average, how many Rwandans were killed per day during the genocide, according to the author?

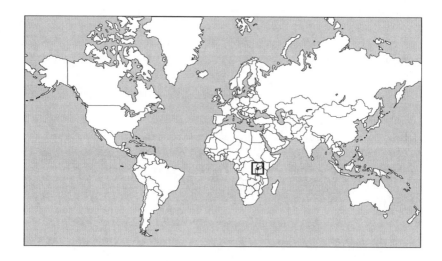

Like the Holocaust of Jews and others during World War II—the scale and shame of the world's inaction during the Rwandan genocide still staggers the mind.

Fifteen years ago today [April 2009], men and women picked up machetes and murdered their neighbors by the hundreds of thousands. And the world watched. The 100-day massacre has since inspired books and Hollywood movies, and left a mark on the global conscience, prompting international campaigns for intervention, such as in Darfur.

But perhaps Rwanda's most enduring legacy is found in the arena of international justice and peacekeeping. In The Hague, [the site of international courts] and other venues, judges, prosecutors, investigators, and activists have begun to bring warlords and despots to justice. And organizations, such as the United Nations [UN] and the African Union, have asserted themselves more. They've sent blue-helmeted battalions of peacekeepers into active war zones, such as Darfur and the Democratic Republic of the Congo (DRC), with stronger mandates to protect civilians.

A Historic Turning Point?

Is international justice and peacekeeping having a deterrent effect on modern despots? That's hard to tell. But many observers still see the Rwandan genocide as a kind of turning point in human history, a chance to change the world.

"We have to be modest and realistic in terms of our expectations of results achieved," says Richard Dicker, who heads the international justice program at Human Rights Watch in New York. "But what we have seen, with the example of the arrest of [former Serbian president] Slobodan Milosevic, with the arrest of former Liberian leader Charles Taylor . . . is a growing, though still fragile, trend toward ending the impunity associated with the commission of crimes against humanity."

War crimes still may occur in war zones, such as Afghanistan, but there are indications that a new standard is developing at the most grassroots level.

Reports have surfaced of Afghan warlords instructing their militia members on what they can, and cannot do, in order to adhere to the Geneva Convention, Mr. Dicker says. Similarly, the DRC has adopted laws that ban the enlistment of child soldiers. And the arrest and pending prosecution of Congolese warlord Thomas Lubanga [Dyilo] in January 2009 sends a signal "that this practice [of using children as soldiers] is a crime under international law, for which there could be prosecution."

Confronting Inaction and Apathy

For John Prendergast, the Rwandan genocide broke the apathy of the 1990s, and gave momentum for an international anti-genocide movement which has forced political leaders, UN agencies and now the International Criminal Court (ICC) to take action before genocide reaches the horrific levels of Rwanda.

"One of the most important developments in international law since the Nuremberg trials [to prosecute war crimes after World War II] has been the creation of the ICC," says Mr. Prendergast, head of the Washington-based anti-genocide group, the Enough Project. "The next decade will be messy as the ICC's initial suspects and indictees at times elude justice. But over time, as more war criminals are brought into custody, a growing shift toward prevention and deterrence will be inevitable. With prosecutions by the [ICC] tribunals for the Rwandan and Yugoslav genocides, as well as the Sierra Leone special court, the tide is definitely shifting in favor of accountability."

Prendergast argues that post-Rwandan activism is already having an effect in war zones such as Darfur. Whereas the Sudanese regime once denied humanitarian access to civilians in its conflict with Southern Sudanese separatists—killing up to 2 million—Sudanese actions in Darfur have killed "only" 300,000, thus far. "Hundreds of thousands of Darfurians are very likely alive today because of the strength of the anti-genocide activist movement," argues Prendergast.

The Pace of Justice

Yet even proponents of international justice say that progress is slow. ICC prosecutors, say some, have been too eager to apply the legal term "genocide" to the conflict in Darfur, and powerful nations have been reluctant to follow through on their own commitments to respond. And while the world sends ever-larger peacekeeping missions to places such as Darfur and the Congo (a nation with no effective government), the peacekeepers themselves are poorly equipped and often told by their own governments to keep their heads down and come home alive.

"After 15 years, the word genocide is being used more and more, but if you take it case by case, I don't think the international community is following up on its commitment to stop genocide from happening," says Guillaume Lacaille, a former political officer with the UN [Organization] Mission in [the Democratic Republic of the] Congo (MONUC) and now a senior researcher at the International Crisis Group in Nairobi.

"In principle, we are eager to send in peacekeeping missions. In reality, very few countries in the developed world are in a position to offer troops. Even with the MONUC, which is the first mission of such a size [17,000 soldiers and police], they are unable to meet any of their obligations, such as citizen protection, training of army troops."

He sighs. "We are reaching the point," he says, "where the peacekeeping tool is going to be broken."

Recollections of a Peacekeeper

Compared with the six-year-long slow burn of conflict in Sudan's Darfur region—which has claimed some 300,000 lives, mainly civilians—the Rwandan genocide was a wildfire driven by prevailing political winds. Moving from house to house, village to village, it took attackers 100 days to kill 800,000 people—an astounding rate of 8,000 people a day, 333 an hour, five per minute.

Phil Lancaster was a peacekeeper in Rwanda at the time, part of a tiny Canadian-led UN observation mission meant to monitor the nascent peace process between the government and the rebel Rwandan Patriotic Front [RPF] of Paul Kagame.

Lancaster's commander, Lt. Gen. Roméo Dallaire, made repeated requests for the UN Security Council to send him more troops and give him a stronger mandate to intervene to protect civilians. Like Dallaire, Mr. Lancaster felt a sickening helplessness as he watched the death toll rise—and Washington [DC] and the UN issue endless appeals for an end to the killing. But unlike General Dallaire, Lancaster does not believe that more and more troops and stronger mandates are necessarily the way to stop a genocide.

"I think we've gone a long way back since Rwanda," says Lancaster. "The ICC is a fine idea, a world court. It has the potential to lend force to direct arguments with leaders that misbehave."

But without a world government to enforce the decisions of that world court, and with many of the major powers, including the United States, refusing to recognize the authority of the ICC, the power of the ICC is compromised.

Darfur Tests International Justice

The ICC's ability to adjudicate cases involving war crimes by top national leaders is now being put to the test, with the ongoing trial of former Liberian president Charles Taylor, who is accused of war crimes both at home and in neighboring Sierra Leone. But critics like Lancaster say the court may have overreached its capacity by issuing an arrest warrant against President Omar al-Bashir of Sudan for war crimes in the Darfur conflict—an arrest warrant that the ICC has no ability to enforce.

Rather than serving as a deterrent against "leaders who misbehave," the ICC may actually have the unintended effect of pushing leaders like President Bashir and rebel leaders like Lord's Resistance Army chief Joseph Kony, into a corner, where brutality against civilians is the only tool they have left to use.

Even worse, he says, there are times when countries such as the Congo decide to set aside differences with an ICC-indicted war criminal, such as Gen. Bosco Ntaganda, and effectively look the other way in return for short-term political cooperation.

For Rwandans themselves, the greatest legacy of the genocide is the 15 years of relative peace that have come during the rule of President Kagame.

Lancaster, who also served in MONUC's disarmament program, says he had a surreal experience a month ago in the Congolese town of Goma, when he saw General Bosco—a man wanted for the deaths of hundreds of civilians in the Congolese region of Ituri—entering a restaurant. "He walks in, with escorts, has lunch with a beautiful view of Lake Kivu, and walks out, without a care in the world," he says. "And this is in Goma, where the greatest concentration of [UN] peace-keepers is found, and MONUC says they don't have the mandate to arrest him."

He pauses in exasperation. "There is a direct conflict between the universal utopian application of the human rights agenda on one hand, and realpolitik on the other."

Ready to Accept Responsibility

For Rwandans themselves, the greatest legacy of the genocide is the 15 years of relative peace that have come during the rule of President Kagame. By African standards, the country has emerged as an economic dynamo: Gross national product surged 11 percent in 2008. But the peace comes at a price of freedom of expression, with most newspapers either state-owned or voicing a pro-Kagame line, and with the ruling RPF party the only political game in town.

Justice at home has been meted out by thousands of traditional "Gacaca" (pronounced ga-cha-cha) courts. These have given individual Rwandan victims an opportunity to confront those who participated in the attacks, and offered some time for social healing to start. But progress and the reach of international justice appears slow for many Rwandans: Top alleged perpetrators—including former ministers and the head of the Hutu rebel movement, the Democratic Forces for the Liberation of Rwanda (FDLR)—remain at large in Europe, in the jungles of eastern DRC, and in the United States.

Guatemala's Narco-War Can Be Traced Back to an Earlier Genocide

Rory Carroll

Rory Carroll is South American correspondent for the Guardian. *In the following viewpoint, he maintains that the widespread narco-violence that has gripped Guatemala can be traced back to a US-orchestrated coup and a government-sponsored genocidal campaign that massacred hundreds of thousands of impoverished Mayan villagers. Carroll points out that the brutality and lawlessness of that era resulted in political and economic instability, widespread corruption, and impunity for criminal gangs. In recent years, drug cartels were able to move in and perpetrate new campaigns of violence, suspicion, and fear.*

As you read, consider the following questions:

1. According to the author, how many people have been killed by narco-fueled violence in the region between 2007 and 2011?

2. How much anti-narcotics aid did Hillary Clinton pledge to the region in June 2011, according to the author?

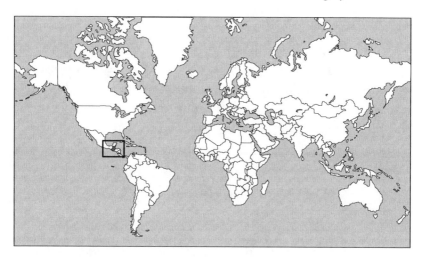

3. What year does the author say that the CIA orchestrated a coup in Guatemala?

It is called a war, but there is no front line or thunder of battle in this scorched wilderness. There is only a no man's land where the dead pile up in silence and the living have nothing to say.

Twenty-seven farm labourers were decapitated and had their heads strewn across a field one recent night [mid-2011], but ask neighbours and they reply with blank looks and apologetic shrugs, as if it happened in a distant land.

Two well-known peasant leaders were killed in separate incidents as if by phantoms. Broad daylight, but no witnesses. Months later, some in the community profess ignorance it even happened. "Ricardo Estrada and Jorge Gutiérrez are dead?"

Yes, they are dead. As are three Mexicans shot in a house last week [June 2011], according to neighbourhood whispers. A pickup spirited away the bodies and the home owner scrubbed the blood before police arrived. They decided nothing happened.

A Brutal War

Welcome to El Naranjo, a sun-blistered one-street town on Guatemala's northern frontier, once in the middle of nowhere, now in the middle of Latin America's drug war. Mexico's narco-fuelled bloodshed, with 36,000 dead in four years, is dripping here and across much of Central America.

The International Commission Against Impunity in Guatemala, a UN-mandated body, said the country risked becoming a narco-state.

The isthmus has been a transit point for Andean cocaine for decades, but its importance to cartels has multiplied since the US Coast Guard shut down alternative Caribbean routes. Competition has sharpened since Mexico's crackdown flushed some narcos south, notably the Zetas, a particularly brutal bunch who seek to annihilate rivals.

The region can ill afford such visitors. Guatemala, Honduras and El Salvador are already world murder capitals because of poverty, youth gangs and dysfunctional, feeble states. Hurricanes and climate change, which disrupt agriculture, do not help. The massacre of the peasants—targeted allegedly because the ranch owner stole Zeta cocaine—has filled the region with foreboding. "This is a war without quarter," Guatemala's president, Álvaro Colom, told the *Guardian*. "There is a lot of infiltration, a lot of corruption. We need a NATO [North Atlantic Treaty Organization]-type force to fight back."

Alarm bells are ringing across the region. General Douglas Fraser, head of US Southern Command, called organised crime Central America's gravest threat. Last week, [US secretary of state] Hillary Clinton pledged $300m [million] in US anti-narcotics aid to the region, an increase of more than 10% from 2010. The International Commission Against Impunity in Guatemala, a UN [United Nations]-mandated body, said the country risked becoming a narco-state.

A Region Ruled by Fear

That has already happened on a local level in Petén, a vast, 2m hectare (5m acre) nature reserve on the border with Mexico that contains rain forest, Mayan ruins—and the marks of interlopers. From the air you see dozens of long, thin gashes in the jungle canopy: airstrips for cocaine-laden planes. The aircraft, worth a small fraction of the cargo's US street value, are so often abandoned there is a cemetery for them.

On the ground you can travel for days without seeing another soul, but when the forest gives way to pasture and bony cattle it means a town is close. El Naranjo is a few hours' bumpy drive from where the peasants were slaughtered. It reeks of fear.

"Don't mention this to anyone here, please," begged one shopkeeper, after casually mentioning that *los pesados* (literally "the heavy ones"), favoured his $130 snakeskin boots. He had inadvertently broken a rule: don't talk about narcos, not even in euphemism. A community leader who requested anonymity said Zetas were forcing people to choose sides, breeding a paralysing suspicion. "There are eyes and ears everywhere." He shook his head. "One of the least populated places on the planet and it's claustrophobic."

Surviving Terror

Community leaders were too nervous to meet UN officials in a nearby municipality. El Naranjo's only journalist, Carlos Jiménez, a one-man radio station, has made a video to be aired if he is murdered. "It names names, says things I can't say in this life."

Nobody trusts phones. "They are tapped so we speak to our people up there in codes," said Ramón Cadena [Rámila], who is based in Guatemala City as Central America director of the International Commission of Jurists. "Terror is multiplied when people know they can be killed and nothing happens afterwards."

A music store reflects El Naranjo's mood: instead of ballads it was playing the sellout CD of an evangelical preacher's hell and damnation sermon: "Pray now, because judgment is upon us!"

An Insider's Look

The town's mayor, José Alfredo Morales, 52, was one of the few to go on the record. Over roast chicken in a deserted diner he detailed how settlers had carved farms out of the jungle 40 years earlier, how guerrillas and government troops spread mayhem in the 1980s, and how criminality exploded after the 1997 peace accords.

As conversation turned to recent events, the restaurant owner stationed himself within earshot but gazed at the street, seemingly oblivious. The mayor started tailoring his answers to the volume of passing traffic. During lulls he talked about the weather and cattle. While pickups rumbled past, sabotaging the eavesdropping, he rattled through more sensitive topics.

The state neglected the region, he said, so *los pesados* traditionally supported the community with infrastructure—roads, churches, clinics—and handouts. Rival groups coexisted more or less in peace until a new group arrived "looking for space"—the mayor extended his elbows in demonstration. "Now they all hate each other. It's got very complicated."

At the end of the interview he raised his voice: "So basically what I'm saying is people are very happy here. It's all very quiet *Todo tranquilo.*"

The Crackdown

El Naranjo is quiet, for now. After the massacre the government declared a temporary "state of siege" in the region, enabling the army to impose a curfew, chase suspects and support the feeble police force. Dozens of vehicles and weapons, including assault rifles and grenades, have been impounded.

About two dozen Zeta suspects have been arrested and paraded before cameras. Well-fed narcos who used to strut around town with pistols on their hips have melted away.

It added up, said President Colom, seated in his palace in Guatemala City, to a crackdown that showed the state could defeat narco-trafficking. "Our resources are limited but we are responding to this very serious threat."

On a laptop he showed air routes, depicted as red lines, shut down with US help, forcing traffickers to use land routes. Authorities were purging corrupt police, bolstering the judicial system and deploying military units to narco hot spots. He suggested the region form "a type of NATO" to fight organised crime.

A Strategy to Confront Narco-Violence

Colom, at times so softly spoken as to be barely audible, asked Europe and the US for more counter-narcotic aid and to rein in cocaine consumption. He lamented rampant money laundering and said Guatemalan elites ducked taxes needed to strengthen governance. "But we are not a failed state. We have a strategy."

In an office overlooking a parade ground with clipped lawns, the defence minister, General Juan José Ruiz, was even more bullish. Two thousand soldiers and 1,000 police were reclaiming Petén from the drug lords, he said. "We are sorting it out. We've caught senior people, seized armed caches."

It would be a similar "success story" to the army's retaking of Alta Verapaz, a region overrun by narcos late last year. That was, to say the least, a bold claim. Days earlier, the remains of Allan Stowlinsky, a kidnapped assistant public prosecutor, were dumped in five black plastic bags around the justice ministry in Cobán, the capital of Alta Verapaz.

A Brutal Legacy

Guatemala was reaping the legacy of chronic lawlessness which left state institutions weak and powerless, said Sebastián El-

Accountability for Past Abuses in Guatemala

Guatemala continues to suffer the effects of the 36-year civil war. A United Nations–sponsored Commission for Historical Clarification (CEH) estimated that as many as 200,000 people were killed during the conflict. The CEH attributed 93 percent of the human rights abuses it documented to state security forces and concluded that the military had carried out "acts of genocide." Very few of those responsible for the grave human rights violations during the civil war have been held accountable. Of the 626 massacres documented by the commission, only three cases have been successfully prosecuted in Guatemalan courts.

Guatemala's first conviction for the crime of enforced disappearance occurred in August 2009, when an ex-paramilitary leader was sentenced to 150 years in prison for his role in "disappearing" individuals between 1982 and 1984. The verdict was made possible by a landmark ruling by the country's constitutional court in July 2009, which established that enforced disappearance is a continuing crime not subject to a statute of limitations so long as the victims are still unknown.

"World Report 2011: Guatemala," Human Rights Watch, 2011.

gueta, a researcher on Central America at Amnesty International. "The current violence has not occurred in a vacuum. Massive human rights violations, war crimes and genocide have gone unpunished. In Guatemala impunity is the norm, justice the exception."

Few in Petén expect the relative calm to last. Mexico's Gulf and Sinaloa cartels still have their proxies in the area and the

Zetas are busy recruiting, said an army colonel in the region. "They are offering very good wages, higher than the competition."

A resident of El Naranjo who served in the army in the 1980s said a former comrade had joined the Zetas and was tasked with recruiting five men. "He offered me 15,000 quetzals (£1,205) per month"—a fortune by local standards. The former conscript said he declined. "Once you're in, you can't get out."

The army has imposed a curfew but the teenage conscripts in khaki who patrol on foot and in pickups have no chance of uprooting a narco-trade rooted in the town's very existence, said one community leader. "It's theatre. Everyone knows *los pesados* are still here."

The Zetas' Terror Campaign

In contrast to "traditional" narcos, who garnered local support by offering basic services and amenities, the Zetas, many of them former members of the Mexican and Guatemalan special forces, prefer to gain control through terror.

They allowed one female labourer to survive the farm massacre so she could bear testimony as a warning to others. The workers were rounded up, she told reporters, and surgically stabbed so they remained alive but could not run. Then one by one, over eight hours, they were interrogated and beheaded.

An atrocity worthy of [1979 war film set during the Vietnam War] *Apocalypse Now*'s Colonel Kurtz, but there is no madness in this tropical realm, just a ruthless, relentless, calculating quest for market share.

Fifty Years of War and Bloodshed

Guatemala was a sleepy backwater until the CIA [US Central Intelligence Agency] orchestrated a coup in 1954 to oust the left-wing government and protect US economic interests. A series of military governments, backed by US aid, battled left-wing guerrillas for decades in what became Latin America's bloodiest civil war.

More than 200,000 people died, mostly impoverished Mayan villagers targeted in a genocidal campaign by government troops and militias. Special forces known as Kaibiles, whose training included biting the heads off chickens, committed numerous atrocities, notably the slaughter of civilians in Dos Erres in 1982.

Peace accords were signed in 1996, [former US president] Bill Clinton apologised for US complicity in the war, and democracy took hold. But Guatemala failed to escape the gun. A feeble state, a corrupt ruling elite, and impunity for criminal gangs, many linked to security forces, produced murder rates that exceed the war-era casualty toll.

Poverty and unemployment are rife. Almost half of children suffer chronic malnutrition, one of the world's highest rates, stunting their growth and mental development.

Areas once ravaged by war are suffering a new wave of violence: Mexico's Zetas, a drug cartel formed by former Mexican special forces, have recruited former Kaibiles and other Guatemalans to wrest control of narco-trafficking routes from established rival cartels.

The Darfur Genocide Has Had a Negative Impact in Chad

Shane Bauer

Shane Bauer is a journalist. In the following viewpoint, he reports that the violence in the Darfur region of Sudan has resulted in environmental devastation in neighboring Chad. Bauer contends that as hundreds of thousands of Sudanese refugees have migrated to Chadian refugee camps across the border, they have put a tremendous strain on resources such as water and firewood. An unfortunate consequence of this increasing competition for resources has been an eruption in violence, especially against Sudanese women.

As you read, consider the following questions:

1. According to the United Nations Development Programme (UNDP), where does Chad rank on the list of the poorest countries in the world?

2. What percentage of Chadians living in provinces bordering Sudan have access to safe drinking water, according to the UNDP report?

3. How many Sudanese does the author say took refuge in East Chad after the onset of the violence?

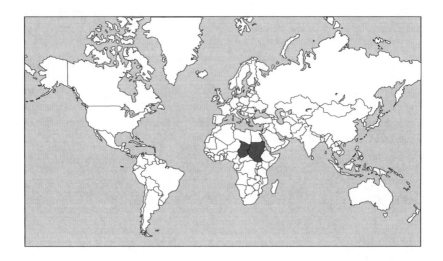

A caravan of a hundred camels traverses the cracked Saharan plains on a several-day journey to the nearest water source in North Darfur as I barrel down the bumpy trail, crammed into the back of a 1960s-model pickup. Stony hills give way to patches of desert, golden grassy meadows, and parched fields of sorghum and millet. Villages of circular huts made of mud and straw are spread thin across the vast, empty countryside, far enough apart to allow the human population to maintain its delicate balance with the scarce resources of their fragile environment.

Many of the villages now look like tiny moonscapes of aboveground craters. The circular mud brick walls of their huts remain standing but their insides are charred and their straw roofs turned to ash. A thin layer of soot coats the cracked clay pots and bed frames that lie exposed to the open sky. Bits of animal bones, scraps of cloth, tin cans, glass, and rusted lanterns are strewn across the ground among empty bullets and one-foot-long mortar shells. Many of the villages remain intact, but they are slowly becoming swept over by sand as they come into their third year of standing empty, their residents having fled as soon as they saw the towers of smoke curling up into the clouds while nearby villages were engulfed in flames.

Sudan and Chad

Separating Sudan's Darfur region and Chad is a 30-foot-wide dried river bed that doubles as a border, but means little for the people living on either side of it. Like all borders in Africa, this one is a product of colonial statecraft, with no relevance to preexisting ethnic identities, linguistic groupings, or communities. Pastoralists move their herds across this unassuming frontier through the lands of their ethnic kin in search of fodder and water. The marauding Janjaweed militia cross into Chad to pillage villages and steal their livestock, while Chadian and Sudanese rebels skip back and forth depending on who and where their enemies are at a given time.

The only people held back by the border are the militaries of either country, so when the Sudanese government waged its genocidal campaign against Darfur's black population, the Masalit, Zaghawa, and other ethnic groups living near the border came to Chad for safety while others fled to closer camps within Darfur. Ishaq Haron, the head of the Treguine refugee camp said, "When we initially fled Sudan, the first people to take care of us were the Chadians." With no international aid agencies present during the first months of ethnic cleansing, he said their kin on the Chadian side of the border offered them food, water, and shelter when they had nowhere else to go.

East Chad may have been better off than Darfur before the war, but only just, and the influx of such a large refugee population put a serious strain on the resource base of Chadians living in the region, and in their ability to sustain themselves. The United Nations Development Programme's (UNDP) 2005 human development report cites Chad as the fifth poorest country in the world, and the eastern region of the country is one of its most remote parts. Aside from the more fertile southern portion of the border region, it is mostly barren and access to water is extremely limited. According to the UNDP report, only two percent of Chadians living in provinces bordering Sudan have access to safe drinking water. Electricity, running water, and telephones are nonexistent outside the provincial capitals, and even in cities their availability is sporadic. People's lives revolve around the collection and consumption of three natural resources: water for drinking and farming, firewood for cooking, and grass for grazing livestock, all of which are scarce.

In East Chad, the deterioration of the environment has already put severe stress on the relations between Chadians and the refugees.

Competition for Resources

The limitation of these natural resources has historically led to conflicts in the region between mostly black sedentary agriculturalists and Arab nomadic pastoralists. Desertification, which has brought about periods of severe drought since the second half of the 20th century, has pushed Arab tribes in Darfur into grazing their livestock on the rich agricultural lands and pastures of the sedentary populations. With the increased pressure of a degrading environment, cattle raids turned into full-fledged conflicts. Then, when armed rebel groups, mostly black Darfuris, rose up demanding that the Sudanese government end the economic marginalization of their people, President Omar al-Bashir took advantage of these preexisting conflicts by arming, financing, and training certain elements of the Arab tribes and using them to target the civilian populations from which these rebels were drawn.

After two million people flooded into camps in Darfur and over 200,000 took refuge in East Chad, the already frail environment quickly began to degenerate. Ouri Cassoni, the largest and northernmost of Chad's 12 refugee camps, is surrounded by nothing but sand and scant shrubbery. The expanse of dusty tents and mud walls that house almost 30,000 people seems to be stuck randomly in the middle of the Chadian desert. During a visit to the camp, UNHCR's [the UN High Commissioner for Refugees'] environmental officer in Chad, Daniel Roger [Tam], said that the environment cannot handle the concentration of so many people in one place. "There are almost thirty thousand refugees in the camp, but no more than five thousand local Chadians in the area," he told me.

Water is in short supply in northeastern Chad, said [Tam], and "there is not enough wood to support the population. The small amount of natural resources [in East Chad] is being overexploited. These refugees also have basic needs to satisfy. They are consuming much more than nature is producing. It has created an imbalance." This imbalance has pushed the environment to the point of crisis, he said, and when environments collapse, everything goes with them. In East Chad, the deterioration of the environment has already put severe stress on the relations between Chadians and the refugees and the more natural resources dwindle, the greater the risk of conflict between refugees and locals becomes. "[Chadians] have the impression that they are being invaded by these people who came from Sudan," said [Tam]. "The main problem is the competition over the exploitation of resources, especially firewood and water."

Women Pay the Price

This competition has led to instances of violent attacks on refugees, and since women are traditionally the ones to collect wood and water, the bulk of the violence has come down on them. Fatima Abu Mohammed, 20-year-old mother of two whose name has been changed for her protection, said that she and other women don't feel free in the camps and she is too afraid to collect wood anymore. Eyes cast down to the sand floor of her shack, she told her story with reservation. "Six months ago I was beaten by a group of men while I was

"Genocide: Enough," cartoon by Steve Greenberg, www.CartoonStock.com. Copyright © Steve Greenberg. Reproduction rights obtainable from www.CartoonStock.com.

searching for wood. There were three of them and they had a gun. Then after they beat me, they raped me."

In Treguine, Haron spoke with poise and self-assurance when talking about the atrocities he and his family were subjected to in Darfur, but as soon as the topic changes to their current situation in the camp, his voice cracked and his eyes began to luster. "In Sudan, the Janjaweed would attack women, beat them, and rape them and here we deal with the same thing."

In an effort to increase the security of women, protect the ecosystem from total collapse, and prevent a new conflict from forming between Chadians and Sudanese refugees, efforts have been made by international NGOs [nongovernmental organizations] to relieve the strain on the environment. UNHCR has dedicated five percent of its budget in Chad to providing Chadian communities near the refugee camps with basic services, especially water facilities. To reduce the rate of deforestation, a new program has been set up at Ouri Cassoni to collect deadwood from designated sites about 20 miles from the camp. Women are taken by vehicles to collect the wood themselves, which is then brought back to be rationed to the entire camp. The rations, however, still fall short of supplying the camps 30,000 people with their requirement of less than two pounds of firewood each. In some of the northern camps where deadwood is most scarce, fuel-efficient, enclosed clay stoves have been built into people's huts as an alternative to the less efficient traditional three-stone fires and in Ouri Cassoni, people are given small amounts of kerosene to supplement their firewood. Refugees have also started to use small-scale kitchen gardens as a sustainable alternative to extensive agriculture in the surrounding areas, using wastewater from domestic activities.

Dealing with Conflict

Natural resources are still diminishing quickly though, and it is only a matter of time before competition erupts into intercommunity conflict. Jessica Hyba, the assistant country director of CARE, a British NGO working on environmental issues in Chad, thinks that the single factor that will determine the stability of East Chad is the length of time that refugees will be there. "In a couple of years' time, should the refugees still be here," she said, "I would imagine that a lot of the peacebuilding activities would probably be around the deadwood collection."

As the sun comes closer to the earth in Ouri Cassoni, I think back over all of the conversations that I have had with refugees about what they suffered in Darfur and the difficulties that they face today in exile. The sky turns grayish yellow and the cone-shaped roofs become silhouettes on the horizon while lone people walk along it, their loose garments fluttering gently in the wind. I struggle to put all the pieces together about Darfur. The conflict only grows in complexity as it continues to expand, pulling Chad further into it. As the environment erodes in East Chad, I wonder how much longer it will be before a new conflict begins. The war in Darfur has sent out ripples of calamity, producing new problems that seem disconnected from the first genocidal intentions. Bombs have fallen on huts and rape used as a weapon, millions have fled and still hope for immediate return, the natural world is being killed, and people wait, hoping that East Chad will be able to hold itself together through it all. In the end, the solution to the looming environmental crisis is the same as that which will stop the escalating conflict in Darfur: an end to the marginalization of the people of Darfur and a just peace that will allow people to return home, and once again spread out across the delicate landscape.

The US War on Drugs Has Led to a Genocide in Mexico

James Petras

James Petras is an author and professor of sociology at Bing-hamton University in New York. In the following viewpoint, he examines the complicity of the US banking system in Mexico's drug trafficking business, pointing out that every major US bank has been involved in laundering hundreds of billions of dollars in drug profits for years. Petras argues that US banks are also responsible for the thousands of Mexicans killed in drug violence. For their role, these banking institutions go unpunished or are given a slap on the wrist, Petras asserts, while Mexico suffers from horrific drug violence.

As you read, consider the following questions:

1. How many Mexicans does the author say have been murdered since 2006?

2. According to US Justice Department records, how much drug money did Wachovia Bank launder between May 1, 2004, and May 31, 2007?

3. According to the author, how much did Wachovia settle for in court for laundering money?

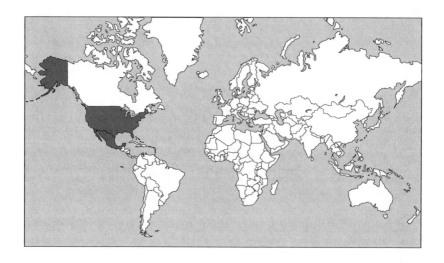

In May 2011, Mexican investigators uncovered another mass clandestine grave with dozens of mutilated corpses; bringing the total number of victims to 40,000 killed since 2006 when the [President Felipe] Calderón regime announced its "war on drug traffickers." Backed by advisers, agents and arms, the White House has been the principal promoter of a "war" that has totally decimated Mexico's society and economy.

If Washington [DC] has been the driving force for the regime's war, Wall Street banks have been the main instruments ensuring the profits of the drug cartels. Every major US bank has been deeply involved in laundering hundreds of billions of dollars in drug profits, for the better part of the past decade.

Mexico's descent into this inferno has been engineered by the leading US financial and political institutions, each supporting "one side or the other" in the bloody "total war" which spares no one, no place and no moment in time. While the Pentagon arms the Mexican government and the US Drug Enforcement Administration [DEA] enforces the "military solution," the biggest US banks receive, launder and transfer hundreds of billions of dollars to the drug lords' accounts, who then buy modern arms, pay private armies of assassins and corrupt untold numbers of political and law enforcement officials on both sides of the border.

Mexico's Descent in the Inferno

Every day scores, if not hundreds, of corpses appear in streets and or are found in unmarked graves; dozens are murdered in their homes, cars, public transport, offices and even hospitals; known and unknown victims in the hundreds are kidnapped and disappear; schoolchildren, parents, teachers, doctors and businesspeople are seized in broad daylight and held for ransom or murdered in retaliation. Thousands of migrant workers are kidnapped, robbed, ransomed, murdered and evidence is emerging that some are sold into the illegal "organ trade." The police are barricaded in their commissaries; the military, if and when it arrives, takes out its frustration on entire cities, shooting more civilians than cartel soldiers. Everyday life revolves around surviving the daily death toll; threats are everywhere, the armed gangs and military patrols fire and kill with virtual impunity. People live in fear and anger.

The Free Trade Agreement: The Sparks That Lit the Inferno

In the late 1980s, Mexico was in crisis, but the people chose a legal way out: They elected a president, Cuauhtémoc Cárdenas, on the basis of his national program to promote the economic revitalization of agriculture and industry. The Mexican elite, led by Carlos Salinas of the Institutional Revolutionary Party (PRI) chose otherwise and subverted the election: The electorate was denied its victory; the peaceful mass protests were ignored. Salinas and subsequent Mexican presidents vigorously pursued a free trade agreement (NAFTA) with the US and Canada, which rapidly drove millions of Mexican farmers, ranchers and small businesspeople into bankruptcy. Devastation led to the flight of millions of immigrant workers. Rural movements of debtors flourished and ebbed, were co-opted or repressed. The misery of the legal economy contrasted with the burgeoning wealth of the traffickers of drugs and people, which generated a growing demand for well-paid armed auxiliaries as soldiers for the cartels. The regional drug syndicates emerged out of the local affluence.

In the new millennium, popular movements and a new electoral hope arose: Andrés Manuel López Obrador (AMLO). By 2006 a vast peaceful electoral movement promised substantial social and economic reforms to "integrate millions of disaffected youth." In the parallel economy, the drug cartels were expanding and benefiting from the misery of millions of workers and peasants marginalized by the Mexican elite, who had plundered the public treasury, speculated in real estate, robbed the oil industry and created enormous privatized monopolies in the communication and banking sectors.

In 2006, millions of Mexican voters were once again denied their electoral victory: The last best hope for a peaceful transformation was dashed. Backed by the US administration, Felipe Calderón stole the election and proceeded to launch the "War on Drug Traffickers" strategy dictated by Washington.

The War Strategy Escalates the Drug War

The massive escalation of homicides and violence in Mexico began with the declaration of a war on the drug cartels by the fraudulently elected President Calderón, a policy pushed initially by the [George W.] Bush administration and subsequently strongly backed by the [Barack] Obama–[Hillary] Clinton regime. Over 40,000 Mexican soldiers filled the streets, towns and barrios—violently assaulting citizens—especially young people. The cartels retaliated by escalating their armed assaults on police. The war spread to all the major cities and along the major highways and rural roads; murders multiplied and Mexico descended further into a Dantesque inferno [referring to Dante Alighieri's epic poem]. Meanwhile, the Obama regime "reaffirmed" its support for a militarist solution on

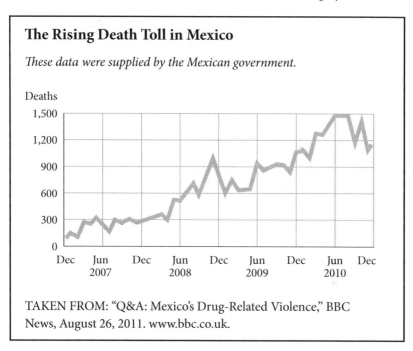

The Rising Death Toll in Mexico

These data were supplied by the Mexican government.

TAKEN FROM: "Q&A: Mexico's Drug-Related Violence," BBC
News, August 26, 2011. www.bbc.co.uk.

both sides of the border: Over 500,000 Mexican immigrants
were seized and expelled from the US; heavily armed border
patrols multiplied. Cross-border gun sales grew exponentially.
The US "market" for Mexican manufactured goods and agricultural products shrank, further widening the pool for cartel
recruits while the supply of high-powered weapons increased.
White House gun and drug policies strengthened both sides in
this maniacal murderous cycle: The US government armed the
Calderón regime and the American gun manufacturers sold
guns to the cartels through both legal and underground arms
sales. Steady or increasing demand for drugs in the US—and
the grotesque profits derived from trafficking and sales—
remained the primary driving force behind the tidal wave of
violence and societal disintegration in Mexico.

Drug profits, in the most basic sense, are secured through
the ability of the cartels to launder and transfer billions of
dollars through the US banking system. The scale and scope
of the US banking–drug cartel alliance surpasses any other

economic activity of the US private banking system. According to US Justice Department records, one bank alone, Wachovia Bank (now owned by Wells Fargo), laundered $378.3 billion dollars between May 1, 2004, and May 31, 2007. Every major bank in the US has served as an active financial partner of the murderous drug cartels—including Bank of America, Citibank, and J.P. Morgan, as well as overseas banks operating out of New York, Miami and Los Angeles, as well as London.

Without US arms and financial services supporting both the illegitimate Mexican regimes and the drug cartels—there could be no "drug war," no mass killings and no state terror.

The Impunity of US Banks

While the White House pays the Mexican state and army to kill Mexicans suspected of drug trafficking, the US Justice Department belatedly slaps a relatively small fine on the major US financial accomplice to the murderous drug trade, Wachovia Bank, spares its bank officials from any jail time and allows major cases to lapse into dismissal.

The major agency of the US Treasury involved in investigating money laundering, the Undersecretary for Terrorism and Financial Intelligence, deliberately ignored the blatant collaboration of US banks with drug terrorists, concentrating almost their entire staff and resources on enforcing sanctions against Iran. For seven years, Treasury Undersecretary Stuart Levey used his power as head of the Department for Terrorism and Financial Intelligence to pursue Israel's phony "war on terrorism" against Iran, rather than shut down Wachovia's money-laundering operations with the Mexican drug terrorists. In this period of time an estimated 40,000 Mexican civilian have been killed by the cartels and the army.

Without US arms and financial services supporting both the illegitimate Mexican regimes and the drug cartels—there could be no "drug war," no mass killings and no state terror. The simple acts of stopping the flood of cheap subsidized US agriculture products into Mexico and decriminalizing the use and purchase of cocaine in the US would dry up the pool of "cartel soldiers" from the bankrupted Mexican peasantry and cut back the profits and demand for illegal drugs in the US market.

The Drug Traffickers, the Banks and the White House

If the major US banks are the financial engines which allow the billion-dollar drug empires to operate, the White House, the US Congress and the law enforcement agencies are the basic protectors of these banks. Despite the deep and pervasive involvement of the major banks in laundering hundreds of billions of dollars in illicit funds, the "court settlements" pursued by US prosecutors have led to no jail time for the bankers. One court's settlement amounted to a fine of $50 million dollars, less than 0.5% of one of the bank's (the Wachovia/Wells Fargo bank) $12.3 billion profits for 2009. Despite the deaths of tens of thousands of Mexican civilians, the US executive branch directed the DEA, the federal prosecutors and judges to impose a laughable "punishment" on Wachovia for its illegal services to the drug cartels. The most prominent economic officials of the Bush and Obama regimes, including [Lawrence] Summers, [Henry] Paulson, [Timothy] Geithner, [Alan] Greenspan, [Ben] Bernanke et al., are all long-term associates, advisers and members of the leading financial houses and banks implicated in laundering the billions of drug profits.

Laundering drug money is one of the most lucrative sources of profit for Wall Street; the banks charge hefty commissions on the transfer of drug profits, which they then lend to borrowing institutions at interest rates far above what—if any—they pay to drug trafficker depositors. Awash in sanitized drug profits, these US titans of the finance world can easily buy their own elected officials to perpetuate the system.

Even more important and less obvious is the role of drug money in the recent financial meltdown, especially during its most critical first few weeks.

According to the head of the United Nations Office on Drugs and Crime, Antonio Maria Costa, "In many instances, drug money (was) . . . currently the only liquid investment capital. . . . In the second half of 2008, liquidity was the banking system's main problem and hence liquid capital became an important factor . . . interbank loans were funded by money that originated from drug trade and other illegal activities . . . (there were) signs that some banks were rescued in that way." Capital flows from the drug billionaires were key to floating Wachovia and other leading banks. In a word: The drug billionaires saved the capitalist financial system from collapse!

The Link Between Banking and Drug Trafficking

By the end of the first decade of the 21st century, it has become clear that capital accumulation, at least in North America, is intimately linked to generalized violence and drug trafficking. Because capital accumulation is dependent on financial capital, and the latter is dependent on the industry profits from the multi-hundred-billion dollar drug trade, the entire ensemble is embedded in the "total war" over drug profits. In times of deep crises the very survival of the US financial system—and through it, the world banking system—is linked to the liquidity of the drug "industry."

At the most superficial level the destruction of Mexican and Central American societies—encompassing over 100 million people—is a result of a conflict between drug cartels and the political regimes of the region. At a deeper level there is a multiplier or "ripple effect" related to their collaboration: The cartels draw on the support of the US banks to realize their profits; they spend hundreds of millions on the US arms industry and others to secure their supplies, transport and markets; they employ tens of thousands of recruits for their vast private armies and civilian networks and they purchase the compliance of political and military officials on both sides of the borders.

For its part, the Mexican government acts as a conduit for US Pentagon/federal police, homeland security, drug enforcement and political apparatuses prosecuting the "war," which has put Mexican lives, property and security at risk. The White House stands at the strategic center of operations—the Mexican regime serves as the frontline executioners.

On one side of the "war on drugs" are the major Wall Street banks; on the other side, the White House and its imperial military strategists and in the "middle" are 90 million Mexicans and 40,000 murder victims and counting.

Relying on political fraud to impose economic deregulation in the 1990s (neoliberalism), the US policies led directly to the social disintegration, criminalization and militarization of the current decade. The sophisticated narco-finance economy has now become the most advanced stage of neoliberalism. When the respectable become criminals, the criminals become respectable.

The issue of genocide in Mexico has been determined by the empire and its "knowing" bankers and cynical rulers.

Periodical and Internet Sources Bibliography

The following articles have been selected to supplement the diverse views presented in this chapter.

Rory Carroll	"Argentinian Founding Father Recast as Genocidal Murderer," *Guardian* (UK), January 13, 2011.
David Dagan	"The Cleanest Place in Africa," *Foreign Policy*, October 19, 2011.
Economist	"The Genocide in Rwanda: The Difficulty of Trying to Stop It Happening Ever Again," April 8, 2009.
Tom Esslemont	"Armenia-Turkey Thaw Tinged with Pain," BBC News, July 4, 2009. http://news.bbc.co.uk.
Henry Green	"Rwandan Genocide: A Survivor's Story," *Guardian* (UK), October 13, 2011.
Saunders Jumah	"Africa, Open Your Eyes," *New Era* (Africa), October 7, 2011.
Guillaume Perrier	"Armenians Peel Back the Layers of a Painful Past," *Guardian* (UK), June 28, 2011.
Isha Sesay and Amanda Sealy	"Rwandan Genocide Survivor Teaches Forgiveness," CNN, March 8, 2011. www.cnn.com.
Sabrina Tavernise and Sebnem Arsu	"Inside the Turkish Psyche: Traumatic Issues Trouble a Nation's Sense of Its Identity," *New York Times*, October 12, 2007.
Sam Thampapillai	"Sri Lanka's Bitter Peace One Year On," *Sydney Morning Herald*, May 20, 2010.

For Further Discussion

Chapter 1

1. Why is defining genocide a contentious and sometimes controversial issue? Use one of the specific situations discussed in this chapter to illuminate your answer.

2. How do you think your country should handle the Armenian genocide? Provide an explanation for your answer.

Chapter 2

1. After reading about current genocides around the world, which do you feel is most pressing? Why?

2. How do you think the media have done in raising awareness on the situations discussed in this chapter? How can they improve?

Chapter 3

1. What is your opinion of the Responsibility to Protect doctrine?

Chapter 4

1. What is your assessment of Rwanda's attempts to deal with the legacy of the horrific 1994 genocide? In what ways is the country succeeding? Failing?

2. How may genocides or sectarian conflicts in one country affect its neighbors?

Organizations to Contact

The editors have compiled the following list of organizations concerned with the issues debated in this book. The descriptions are derived from materials provided by the organizations. All have publications or information available for interested readers. The list was compiled on the date of publication of the present volume; the information provided here may change. Be aware that many organizations take several weeks or longer to respond to inquiries, so allow as much time as possible.

Amnesty International (AI)
5 Penn Plaza, 16th Floor, New York, NY   10001
(212) 807-8400 • fax: (212) 627-1451
e-mail: admin-us@aiusa.org
website: www.amnesty.org

Established in 1961, Amnesty International (AI) is one of the premier independent human rights organizations in the world. AI is made up of 2.8 million members, supporters, and activists who work together to address human rights abuses in more than 150 countries and territories. AI members and activists mobilize letter-writing campaigns, mass demonstrations, vigils, and direct lobbying efforts on behalf of individuals and groups being oppressed, tortured, and imprisoned for political, economic, social, or cultural reasons. Every year AI publishes the influential *State of the World's Human Rights* report, which assesses the global state of human rights. It also publishes monthly e-newsletters, *Stop Violence Against Women* and *Counter Terror with Justice.*

Genocide Intervention Network
1025 Connecticut Avenue NW, Suite 310
Washington, DC   20036
(202) 559-7405 • fax: (202) 559-7410
e-mail: info@genocideintervention.net
website: www.genocideintervention.net

The Genocide Intervention Network is an organization dedicated to empowering individuals and communities with strategies to prevent genocide. In 2005 the Genocide Intervention Network was established to fight the horrific genocide in Darfur. Since that time, it has broadened its mission to help people and communities in other areas, including Burma and the Democratic Republic of the Congo. One of its main areas of action is legislation; the Genocide Intervention Network lobbies the US Congress and the international community to encourage policy makers to be more proactive in recognizing and fighting genocide. The organization's website features access to an e-mail newsletter, which provides updates on recent initiatives and breaking news. There is also a blog chronicling current events and developing areas of concern.

Genocide Watch
PO Box 809, Washington, DC   20044
(202) 643-1405
e-mail: communications@genocidewatch.org
website: www.genocidewatch.org

Genocide Watch is an international coalition that works to recognize, track, stop, and punish genocide, war crimes, and other forms of mass murder. It is dedicated to raising awareness on the issue and building an agile and formidable international movement to prevent genocide. The organization analyzes high-risk situations around the world to predict the chances for genocidal acts and then works to raise awareness of the problem. Genocide Watch's website has an extensive archive of information on past genocides; it also features the Cambodia Project, which offers updates on bringing the perpetrators of the Pol Pot genocide to justice.

Human Rights First
333 Seventh Avenue, 13th Floor, New York, NY   10001-5108
(212) 845-5200 • fax: (212) 845-5299
e-mail: feedback@humanrightsfirst.org
website: www.humanrightsfirst.org

Human Rights First is an independent international human rights organization that advances human rights through accurate research and reporting on human rights abuses worldwide, advocacy for victims, and coordination with other human rights organizations. The group is focused in five key areas: crimes against humanity, fighting discrimination, aiding human rights activists, refugee protection, and advocating for fair legal protections. To that end, Human Rights First offers a series of in-depth studies on such issues, including recent reports on anti-Semitism in Europe, oppressive government counterterrorist measures in Uzbekistan, and China's role in the Sudanese conflict. It also provides an e-newsletter, *Rights Wire*, which examines topical issues in the human rights field.

Human Rights Watch (HRW)

350 Fifth Avenue, 34th Floor, New York, NY   10118-3299
(212) 290-4700 • fax: (212) 736-1300
website: www.hrw.org

Founded in 1978, Human Rights Watch (HRW) is a nonprofit, independent human rights group that researches and publishes more than one hundred reports to shed light on pressing human rights abuses. Often working in difficult situations—including those controlled by oppressive and tyrannical governments—HRW strives to provide accurate and impartial reporting on human rights conditions for the media, financial institutions, and international organizations. HRW is often on the front lines in situations where genocidal campaigns begin and provide much-needed information on crimes and abuses. The group's wide-ranging and thorough reports can be accessed on the HRW website. Interested viewers can also access video, audio, podcasts, photo essays, and photo galleries on the site.

Institute for the Study of Genocide (ISG)

John Jay College of Criminal Justice
899 Tenth Avenue, Room 325, New York, NY   10019
e-mail: info@instituteforthestudyofgenocide.org
website: www.instituteforthestudyofgenocide.org

The Institute for the Study of Genocide (ISG) is an independent, nonprofit organization chartered by the University of the State of New York that promotes a greater understanding of "the causes, consequences, and prevention of genocide." Located at the John Jay College of Criminal Justice, the center was established in 1982 to study and raise awareness of the problem of genocide around the world. ISG conducts extensive policy analyses; hosts scholarly conferences to exchange information and coordinate efforts; works with refugee and human rights organizations; and consults with local, regional, and national governments. It also provides information to media organizations and publishes the *ISG Newsletter* twice a year.

International Association of Genocide Scholars (IAGS)
website: www.genocidescholars.org

The International Association of Genocide Scholars (IAGS) is an international, nonprofit membership organization that aims to further research on genocide and promote policy studies on the prevention of genocide. IAGS hosts meetings and conferences to disseminate and discuss new research and policy analyses with the ultimate goal of more effectively predicting and preventing genocide. IAGS publishes *Genocide Studies and Prevention: An International Journal,* which provides a forum for international scholars and raises awareness of the issue.

International Institute for Genocide
& Human Rights Studies
255 Duncan Mill Road, Suite 310, Toronto, ON   M3B 3H9
(416) 250-9807 • fax: (416) 512-1736
e-mail: admin@GenocideStudies.org
website: www.genocidestudies.org

The International Institute for Genocide & Human Rights Studies is an academic center that was established to provide research and education in the field of genocide studies. The institute maintains that through the study of past genocides, such as the Holocaust, society can better predict, prevent, and help the victims of present and future genocidal campaigns. Its website features press releases, news reports, and articles on the topic of genocide.

Society for Threatened Peoples
PO Box 2024, D-37010 Gottingen, Geiststrasse 7
Gottingen   D-37073
   Germany
+49-551-49906-0 • fax: +49-551-58028
e-mail: info@gfbv.de
website: www.gfbv.de

The Society for Threatened Peoples is an independent human rights group that vows to live by the motto: "Not turning a blind eye." With the help of individual members, the organization develops and implements human rights campaigns all over the world, such as putting an end to slavery in Mauritania; aiding the Maasai people to keep their land in Africa; and releasing Bahá'í prisoners in Iran. It also researches reports and studies on pressing human rights issues. The Society for Threatened Peoples website offers links to publications, including *GfbV* magazine, which provides updated information on recent genocidal campaigns.

Stop Genocide Now (SGN)
1732 Aviation Boulevard #138, Redondo Beach, CA   90278
e-mail: iact-info@stopgenocidenow.org
website: www.stopgenocidenow.org

Stop Genocide Now (SGN) is an international community of volunteers who work to prevent genocide in troubled areas around the world. SGN is dedicated to raising awareness of the horrors of genocide by educating the media, public, and policy makers on the tragic consequences of genocidal campaigns on communities, families, and individuals. Advocacy is also one of SGN's key goals, and members promote more effective ways to address and prevent genocide and help the victims of genocidal campaigns. SGN works extensively in refugee camps to aid men, women, and children displaced by genocide. On the SGN website, there is a blog that offers information on recent initiatives and campaigns, as well as breaking news on situations worldwide. Current news and updates can also be found in the *i-ACTzine*, a magazine that focuses on the SGN efforts worldwide.

UN Human Rights Council

Palais des Nations, Geneva 10   CH-1211
  Switzerland
22 917 9220
e-mail: InfoDesk@ohchr.org
website: www2.ohchr.org

Part of the United Nations (UN), the Human Rights Council is made up of forty-seven member states and focuses on strengthening and protecting human rights around the globe. The council is tasked with making recommendations on some of the most pressing human rights situations today. It works closely with other bodies within the United Nations in addition to national and local governments, nongovernmental organizations, and human rights activists. Transcripts and video of the council's sessions can be found on the group's website, which also features current news and information on recent reports and proceedings.

Bibliography of Books

Alex Alvarez | *Genocidal Crimes.* New York: Routledge, 2010.

Nancy Billias and Leonhard Praeg, eds. | *Creating Destruction: Constructing Images of Violence and Genocide.* New York: Rodopi, 2011.

Claudia Card | *Confronting Evils: Terrorism, Torture, Genocide.* New York: Cambridge University Press, 2010.

Gina Chon and Sambath Thet | *Behind the Killing Fields: A Khmer Rouge Leader and One of His Victims.* Philadelphia: University of Pennsylvania Press, 2010.

Phil Clark | *The Gacaca Courts, Post-Genocide Justice and Reconciliation in Rwanda: Justice Without Lawyers.* New York: Cambridge University Press, 2010.

Lee Ann Fujii | *Killing Neighbors: Webs of Violence in Rwanda.* Ithaca, NY: Cornell University Press, 2009.

Daniel Jonah Goldhagen | *Worse than War: Genocide, Eliminationism, and the Ongoing Assault on Humanity.* New York: PublicAffairs, 2009.

David A. Hamburg | *Preventing Genocide: Practical Steps Toward Early Detection and Effective Action.* Boulder, CO: Paradigm Publishers, 2010.

Alexander Laban Hinton and Kevin Lewis O'Neill, eds.	*Genocide: Truth, Memory, and Representation.* Durham, NC: Duke University Press, 2009.
Adam Jones, ed.	*Evoking Genocide: Scholars and Activists Describe the Works That Shaped Their Lives.* Toronto, ON: Key Publishing House, 2009.
Adam Jones	*Gender Inclusive: Essays on Violence, Men, and Feminist International Relations.* New York: Routledge, 2009.
Adam Jones	*Genocide: A Comprehensive Introduction.* New York: Routledge, 2011.
Ben Kiernan	*The Pol Pot Regime: Race, Power, and Genocide in Cambodia Under the Khmer Rouge, 1975–79.* New Haven, CT: Yale University Press, 2008.
Richard A. Koenigsberg	*Nations Have the Right to Kill: Hitler, the Holocaust, and War.* Elmhurst, NY: Library of Social Science, 2009.
René Lemarchand, ed.	*Forgotten Genocides: Oblivion, Denial, and Memory.* Philadelphia: University of Pennsylvania Press, 2011.
Kristen Renwick Monroe	*Ethics in an Age of Terror and Genocide: Identity and Moral Choice.* Princeton, NJ: Princeton University Press, 2012.
René Provost and Payam Akhavan, eds.	*Confronting Genocide.* New York: Springer, 2011.

William A. Schabas — *Genocide in International Law: The Crime of Crimes*. New York: Cambridge University Press, 2009.

Adam M. Smith — *After Genocide: Bringing the Devil to Justice*. Amherst, NY: Prometheus Books, 2009.

Ervin Staub — *Overcoming Evil: Genocide, Violent Conflict, and Terrorism*. New York: Oxford University Press, 2011.

Gerard Toal and Carl Dahlman — *Bosnia Remade: Ethnic Cleansing and Its Reversal*. New York: Oxford University Press, 2011.

Samuel Totten, ed. — *Plight and Fate of Women During and Following Genocide*. New Brunswick, NJ: Transaction Publishers, 2009.

Samuel Totten and Paul R. Bartrop, eds. — *The Genocide Studies Reader*. New York: Routledge, 2009.

Samuel Totten and Robert K. Hitchcock, eds. — *Genocide of Indigenous Peoples*. New Brunswick, NJ: Transaction Publishers, 2011.

James A. Tyner — *War, Violence, and Population: Making the Body Count*. New York: Guilford Press, 2009.

Alan Wolfe — *Political Evil: What It Is and How to Combat It*. New York: A.A. Knopf, 2011.

Index

Geographic headings and page numbers in **boldface** refer to viewpoints about that country or region.